GHOST INVESTIGATOR

Volume III

Written by
Linda Zimmermann

A
Spirited
Books
Publication

Also by Linda Zimmermann

Bad Astronomy
Forging A Nation
Civil War Memories
Ghosts of Rockland County
Haunted Hudson Valley
More Haunted Hudson Valley
Haunted Hudson Valley III
A Funny Thing Happened on the Way to Gettysburg
Rockland County: Century of History
Mind Over Matter
Home Run
Ghost Investigator, Volume 1: Hauntings of the Hudson Valley
Ghost Investigator, Volume 2: From Gettysburg, PA to Lizzie Borden, AX

The author is always looking for new ghost stories. If you would like to share a haunting experience go to:

www.ghostinvestigator.com

Or write to:

Linda Zimmermann
P.O. Box 192
Blooming Grove, NY 10914

Or send email to:
lindazim@frontiernet.net

Cover Art by David Hamilton

Ghost Investigator: Volume 3
Copyright © 2003 Linda Zimmermann

ISBN: 0-9712326-2-8

Introduction

Ghost Investigator: Volume 3 is the sixth in a series of ghost books I've written. At this point, I can't help but think back to the moment I decided to write the first one, *Ghosts of Rockland County*, and wondered where I would ever find enough stories to fill an entire book!

Years later, I continue to be amazed by the number of haunted places. Rather than being a rarity, ghosts almost seem likely to be present in just about any place that is old or has been touched by some tragedy. By example, the stories in this book range from houses that were built in the eighteenth and nineteenth centuries, to recent and new houses. In the cases of the older structures, it is the long history of human habitation that has put them in the realm of the haunted. In the case of newer houses, it is usually the ground upon which they are built—that is, their proximity to some type of sudden or tragic death.

Several stories are unlike any I have written about before, and illustrate important points. One involves the home of Roxanne Wentworth in Wappingers Falls, NY, who brought home some very solid objects from a cemetery, and a lot more ethereal things in the process. It was reminiscent of the Wershing house in Summit, NJ, (see *Ghost Investigator: Volume 1*) where Mr. Wershing had filled a room with bones and artifacts he had excavated from Indian burial grounds, and suffered the consequences. It's always best to leave funereal objects and the dead where they were laid to rest.

I also had the opportunity to investigate a section of a former mental hospital. I have investigated cemeteries, prisons and abandoned buildings, but never felt anything like I did in the old wards that once housed the incurably insane. Those souls knew the true depths of human suffering, and the imprint of such torment is at least as pronounced and disturbing as any murder or suicide.

This book also contains two stories involving children and their "imaginary friends." Children are particularly sensitive to the spirit world, and while they certainly have fertile imaginations, don't be so certain that they aren't seeing something very real—and very dead.

As I write these words, I still have a long list of places to investigate, and there truly seems to be no end to the bizarre and unearthly activity resulting from human misery and suffering. If one thing has changed over the past several years, it's that it becomes harder with every case to remain completely objective. When you learn the stories of the people behind the hauntings, and come into contact with the residue of their strong emotions, it's impossible not to become involved—on many different levels.

Of course, my primary goal is still to gather hard facts and scientific evidence, but ignoring my own heart and intuition would be to deny other tools that may prove to be of use. An important example of this is illustrated in the first story. Call it a hunch, intuition or whatever you want, but something I felt and believed about the case turned out to be true. It is one of the most fascinating stories I've worked on, and no one yet has failed to feel a chill when learning of it.

This first story is also important for another reason. Frequently, to protect the privacy of everyone involved, I change the names of both the witnesses and the deceased. I have also done that in this case, and I have left out some of the more poignant and revealing details to further prevent the identification of those that have passed. I do not intend to ever sensationalize anyone's personal tragedy, and the essential facts of this case are more than sufficient to expose the startling picture.

Some people have actually gotten upset with me when I have refused to reveal exact names, addresses, and even phone numbers, but that's just plain tough. Privacy is always my first and foremost concern.

So with that, I will leave you to the stories. This book may now be completed, but there are many other ghosts to investigate…

Linda Zimmermann
July 2003

CONTENTS

Lawrence

Have you ever spent hours working on a jigsaw puzzle only to find that there are pieces missing so you cannot complete the picture? Well, that's what it is like most of the time in the ghost investigation world. You can gather dozens of eyewitness accounts from generations of people, collect stacks of videotapes, photographs, and sound recordings, and despite the mountain of ghostly evidence, never have a single clue as to who or what might be responsible for the haunting. Then you hit upon a case where all the pieces come together and you realize it's moments like this that keep you motivated.

This story begins in a house that was built in the early 1960s in Chester, New York. The family who lived there never had any problems, and over the decades a typical suburban development grew up around them. Simultaneously, something else was growing—a cemetery which pushed its borders to the edge of the development. By the time the original owners had retired to Florida and their granddaughter and her husband were moving into the house in 1999, fresh burials were taking place within sight of their home.

Unlike some couples just getting started, Susan and Tony were not strangers in the neighborhood, so there was not that adjustment period of trying to get comfortable and familiar with their surroundings. In addition, Tony was a law enforcement officer in the area, so there was that added feeling of security. Unfortunately, that safe and secure feeling did not last long.

One night when Tony was working the midnight shift, there was a terrible banging noise on the metal doors that led into the basement, right under Susan's bedroom window. She immediately called her husband who was there within minutes, but no evidence could be found of an attempted break-in. It was an alarming beginning to what had promised to be a tranquil life in the family home, where there had never been any incidents of this type.

On another night, Susan, her cousin, and a friend were watching television in the living room. One of her cats—a black one, who never makes an appearance when guests are in the house—showed up in the doorway between the living room and the kitchen. There was a panicked look in the cat's face and his body was tense with fear.

1

Suddenly he hissed as if being threatened, and took off running down the hall, away from the kitchen. A second later the three women heard the back screen door that leads to the kitchen open. Then the wooden door opened, and then both doors promptly slammed shut. Believing an intruder had just entered the house, the three women ran into the kitchen to confront him. No one was there. They ran outside and searched the yard and road, but no one could be found, and no one would have had the time to get out of sight.

The metal basement door where the banging noises first began.

Tony also had an experience with the phantom intruder. One night he was awakened about 1am by unusual sounds outside. Then he heard the back doors being forcefully opened. Racing into the kitchen, he found the doors—which he had securely locked himself—now standing wide open. Once again, a search produced no suspects, and no explanations.

This inability to keep locked doors closed also presented itself when Tony and Susan were away on vacation. Susan's father stopped by to check on things and found that the sliding doors to the patio were standing wide open. Nothing had been broken, there were no signs that the locks had been tampered with, and nothing was missing from the house. On another occasion, Susan came home to find a kitchen window open, and its screen carefully removed and placed against a wall. One of her cats—the black one again—was found outside, cowering under a bush. Both of her cats are house cats, and never go outside, so it must have been something extreme to drive the poor cat out of the window.

As time passed, strange noises could be heard in the basement. They became so frequent, and were heard by so many family members and friends, that it became kind of a joke that some of the men from a local homeless shelter had taken up residence in their basement. Time and time again they searched for the source of the noises, but always found all of the doors locked, and no indications that any animals or humans had been down there. So, if you can rule out anything living, that only leaves one option—the dead.

"I called my mother late one night and told her we had a ghost and I didn't want to live here anymore," Susan said. "But she just thought I was crazy, because she had grown up in this house and had never had anything unusual happen. And my grandparents said that nothing ever happened to them either. But I just knew that we had a ghost."

The situation wasn't a complete mystery, however. Susan realized that the beginning of the intense paranormal activity in the house coincided with two events that occurred close together in 2000—the birth of her son, Tommy, and the tragic death of her elderly neighbor, Sam. In fact, the night Sam died, Tommy's baby monitor picked up the transmission from the old man's monitor, and they heard the final moments of his life. While Susan didn't believe that the frail, gentle little man was responsible for the pounding noises and slamming

3

doors, she couldn't help but feel that Sam's passing somehow opened a door to other spirits. And much of that new activity now centered on her son.

There were times that his room would get icy cold, and the television would turn itself on. Even more fascinating were the stations that would be playing—it would always be one of the two religious channels. Whenever they allowed their son to watch television in his room, it was always and only the cartoon channel, so even if there was some electronic glitch that caused the television to turn on, it should have turned on to cartoons, not the sermons and prayers.

Tommy's room. The television is in the far right corner, and the bed is in the left corner near the door, so it is impossible for him to accidentally turn on the TV.

One evening Susan's friend, Lisa, was going down the hall to the bathroom, and looked in on Tommy. The room was dark and Tommy was fast asleep. When she left the bathroom a few minutes later, she could see lights flickering in his room. Puzzled, she took another look and saw that an electronic Mickey Mouse jester hat had somehow turned itself on and its bright colored lights were flashing. Tommy was still sound asleep, and the hat was high up on a shelf that the little toddler could never reach.

As interesting as blinking lights and religious channels are, the really fascinating part of the story began when Tommy started saying his first words. Susan's cousin, Ann, was babysitting Tommy one

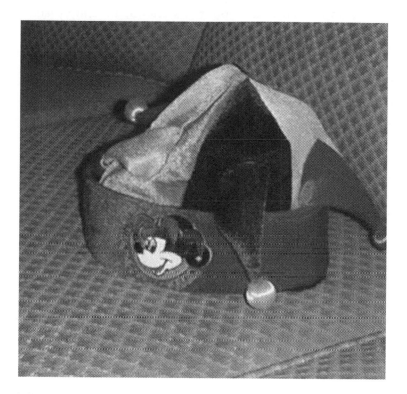

This Mickey Mouse hat has blinking lights at the tips. There is a switch inside that has to be pressed to turn it on.

night, and she was listening to his fledging attempts at the English language. He only knew a handful of basic words beyond mommy and daddy, but that didn't seem to prevent him from carrying on an unintelligible conversation with some imaginary friend. Not expecting an answer, Ann casually asked, "Who are you talking to, Tommy?"

"Lawrence," the boy promptly replied.

Ann was startled by the clear and unusual response, and couldn't wait to ask Susan where he picked up that uncommon name in his tiny vocabulary. No one in the family had any clue as to how the little boy came to have an imaginary friend named Lawrence, as there was no one in their circle of acquaintances with such a name. It was also interesting that he specifically stated Lawrence, as opposed to Larry, which would have been the typical abbreviated version. Over the following months, Tommy's conversations grew in length and complexity, and when asked about his friend, he simply stated that Lawrence was a man who came to visit him. There was nothing frightening about the man, and the boy thought nothing about having a friend only he could see.

However, as the boy got a little older, he began to understand that things like televisions shouldn't turn on by themselves, and men appearing out of thin air in his bedroom was not something normal. Finally one evening, he ran into the living room from his bedroom. His face was pale, his eyes were wide and he started yelling that there was a ghost in his room. Even at such a tender age, his mind had become aware of the difference between the living and the dead.

The question then became whether the adults could now make themselves aware of just what was going on. In October of 2002, Ann had been listening to the live radio broadcast at Smalley's Inn (see page 10), and after reading my books, suggested to Susan that she contact me. I received an email from Susan with a few details, I asked some questions, and my curiosity about the case quickly intensified—especially when I learned about Lawrence, and the fact that a cemetery was close to the house. My next question was whether anyone named Lawrence was buried nearby, as I had that persistent little tickle of intuition on the back of my neck. In fact, I was ready to bet some of my best ghost hunting meters that there would be a grave to match the name, and there would also be some other connection to the case.

And oh, is it ever so gratifying when things actually turn out as predicted!

As soon as I arrived at Susan's house, she told me about the discovery she made just the day before. She went to explore the cemetery with Ann and Lisa, and with row upon row of gravestones, it appeared to be a daunting task. However, as she walked along the edge of the cemetery, reading the names on the very first row of stones, she tripped on something hard. Looking down, she saw that her foot had caught on a small plaque mounted flat in the ground. And on that plaque, was engraved the name Lawrence! Beneath the name was the date of death, 1999, the year they had moved into the house!

While the discovery was startling, it still didn't offer any proof that this Lawrence, who was only in his thirties when he died, was the same young man visiting her son. Determined to find out more, they searched the Internet for Lawrence's obituary. To their astonishment, they found out that Lawrence had been related to Sam, the neighbor whose death seemed to initiate the haunted activity! All of the pieces of the puzzle suddenly snapped together. Someone once said that there's no such thing as coincidences, and in this case I can't agree more.

Lawrence's simple grave marker. I obscured the actual name and inscription in this photo to protect the family's privacy, and left only the year of death.

Buoyed by the excitement of the news, I was eager to begin my investigation. Of course, our first stop had to be the cemetery. It was somewhat chilling standing next to Lawrence's grave, wondering if the spirit that once inhabited the body beneath our feet still walked the earth. Yet, as unsettling as that was, Susan brought my attention to something possibly even sadder.

A few feet from Lawrence's humble plaque on the ground, stands the large, elaborately carved gravestone of his brother, who had died in an accident several years earlier. Around this fancy stone, loved ones have placed all kinds of objects and mementos, like a small shrine. One cannot help wondering why so much attention was lavished on one son, while the other has the barest of nameplates. Of course, there could be countless reasons for this—including Lawrence's own wishes—but this certainly wouldn't be the first family to have alienated one of its members. Without knowing the entire story, it is still sad to see two brothers, both lost in the prime of life, lying together, but unequal, at least in outward appearance.

Standing between the brothers' graves was a sobering experience, and one more reminder that ghosts are not amusements; they are the result of human tragedy and suffering. I hoped that by understanding and acknowledging that fact, we would be able to do more than gather evidence on this restless spirit, we would also help it find peace.

When we returned to the house, I started checking out every nook and cranny for signs of unusual EMF readings or temperatures. There was nothing out of the ordinary. When it grew dark enough, I set up the infrared camcorder in Tommy's room. Nothing appeared. After about an hour, I suggested that Tommy go inside his room, to see if anything might happen then.

Susan took Tommy in his dark room, which he didn't seem to mind, and they both sat on the floor. Very soon after, a few of those mysterious little white spots zipped into the room. Several made an appearance in the span of just a few minutes, which was particularly unusual given the fact that nothing had happened during all the time I had been taping prior to that. The most curious thing of all, however, was when the brightest and largest spot shot across the room, just seconds after I mentioned the name Lawrence.

Almost immediately, Tommy became frightened of the dark, and practically ran out of the room. We tried again a few minutes later, but the little boy was still afraid and I knew it was time to stop. Yet, even though there was not much evidence gathered that night, I considered the results of this case to be a success.

There were two deaths and a birth that coincided with the onset of activity. There was a name that matched a grave. There were numerous eyewitnesses over the course of several years. There was a television that turned itself on and tuned in to religious channels. There was something that didn't allow locked doors to prevent it from gaining entrance into the house. And there was a little boy who had an imaginary friend, who just might be a very real ghost.

Despite the remarkable links found in this case, it will never be closed. It will remain open as long as restless spirits still visit the house, searching for something in death that they did not have in life. While I could not help but be excited by the details of this case, it is ultimately a very sad experience to become involved in this type of situation, and all it implies for those who have not yet found peace.

While I may not conduct any further investigations on the house, I may take the time on occasion to visit a certain grave marked only by a simple plaque. Although I never met the man in life, and know precious little about him, perhaps a flower and a few kind thoughts will bring some comfort, no matter where he is now.

Smalley Inn

In October of 2002, I received a call from Andre from the Woodman's show on the K104 radio station in Putnam County, New York. A couple of years earlier, Andre and some crew members had accompanied me to the haunted Peach Grove Inn in Warwick, New York, for a live broadcast (see the story in *Ghost Investigator, Volume 1*). During the Halloween season of 2002, their live broadcasts were being conducted at a number of haunted locations, but one in particular was worth revisiting, so Andre asked if I could meet them there in a couple of days. Since my October schedule is always brutal, I didn't look forward to getting up at 4am for the investigation, but I couldn't resist after Andre told me some of the details.

In 1852, James J. Smalley bought a hotel in Carmel, New York. In addition to running his hotel, he also served at various times as the local sheriff, coroner and treasurer, until his death in 1867. The area had some tragic history, including a deadly fire, and the execution of a murderer. Eighteen-year-old George Denny had killed 80-year-old Abraham Wanzer with a shotgun blast, and on July 26, 1844 at 5pm, Denny was brought to the gallows erected across the street from the hotel that would become Smalley's, and was put to death in front of a crowd of 4,000 people. It was the only hanging in the county's history.

Smalley Inn

Anthony Porta bought Smalley's in 1968 and operated it as a restaurant and tavern. His son, Tony, Jr., has been managing the place for the last twenty years. Due to a long series of inexplicable events, Tony contacted K104 and told them it just might be a place worth investigating. That was an understatement. When Andre and the other members of the station were there, they heard footsteps, recorded a sound like the creaking of a heavy rope swinging from the ceiling (perhaps from a hanging?), Andre was physically grabbed, lights went out and something pinned Brook Douglas against the bar with such force that it took both Tony and Andre to pry him loose. It all sounded too good to miss.

I arrived at the radio station one chilly October morning about 5:30am. Woodman played the tape of the creaking sound, and it was truly creepy, for lack of a suitable technical term. We waited for a while until the entire "hunting party" was gathered—three people from the station, two reporters and a photographer from the Times Herald Record, and a journalism student from SUNY New Paltz. Of course, it's always best to investigate with as few people as possible to minimize noise and disruptions, but I had a feeling this group was going to make for one wild ghost hunt!

Before describing the investigation that took place that morning, which was wilder than I could have imagined, it's important to know all that has been taking place at Smalley's over the past few years. One of the most unique phenomena occurs with the telephones, and it all began fifteen years ago because of an experiment with a Ouija board. Tony's friend Mike brought over the board to see if they could get some answers to the strange sights and sounds that so many people had been experiencing.

Tony, Mike, and a couple of friends sat in the basement and began by asking the board if anyone from the spirit world was there. A name was spelled out—a man's name that no one recognized but Tony. A few years earlier, a troubled young employee had committed suicide, and his name had been exactly spelled out on the Ouija board. Equally unnerving, was that while the men were using the board, they kept hearing the distinct sound of coins dropping on the floor. While there didn't appear to be any explanation, Tony recalled that this boy had owed him money, and always promised to pay him back.

11

The Ouija board then kept insisting that they should go and unlock the liquor room. Tony couldn't understand that, as he never locked that door. When the board persisted, however, they went over to it and found the door to the liquor room closed and locked with a padlock! With some trepidation, they removed the lock and opened the door. Nothing unusual was inside, but it was unnaturally cold. They left the door open and returned to the Ouija board to ask more questions.

They asked the boy if he had left the liquor room and was now somewhere in the bar or restaurant. The reply was startling. "I am sitting next to Tony," the board spelled out. As unnerving as it was, they kept going, and the board began spelling another word.

P...H...O...N...and then the phone rang in the kitchen. Mike went upstairs to answer it, but no one was there. No sooner did he get back, then the pay phone rang in the bar. Tony went to answer it and no one was there, just some odd static. When they went back to the board, it slowly but repeatedly spelled out just two letters, "H...A...H...A...H...A..."

"He was laughing at us," Tony recalled. "And Mike was really starting to freak out. And when the board then said that there were 'Nine of us ready to play,' that was it. Mike left the board and ran out. I made him come back later and take it away. And you know, after that day he had two years of the worst luck. Everything bad started happening to that guy."

While no more Ouija boards have been used in Smalley's since that day, the mysterious ringing phones have continued. Usually it is the pay phone in the bar that rings, and whoever answers it is greeted only by that odd static. However, one busy night, all the phones got into the act. On a Wednesday night, at exactly 10:33pm, every cell phone and house phone in the place started ringing—and all the calls came from inside, although no one actually placed the calls!

"The kitchen rang the upstairs phone and the upstairs phone rang the pay phone," Tony explained, "the pay phone called the bartender's phone, the bartender's phone called my wife and my wife's called mine. We didn't know what to think. It was the craziest thing and it didn't make any sense. How could all these phones be calling each other without anyone touching them?"

The pay phone in the bar that receives the mysterious calls.

Perhaps the young employee who took his own life is trying to stay in touch with Tony and the employees who were like a second family to him. It seems that suicide victims always have the deepest regrets, and make the saddest and most pitiful attempts to literally reconnect with the life they themselves cut short.

However, that wasn't the end of the bizarre phenomena that night. As Tony went to lock up, the outside door suddenly slammed itself shut and the key was thrown out of the keyhole.

"Someone had shoved it from the inside. It's like whatever it was, was saying, 'Good. Get out.'"

About twelve years ago, Tony's father had an interesting encounter in the upstairs bedroom. He was awakened one night as he felt the weight of someone getting on the bed next to him. He remained still because he believed it was an intruder who might try to harm him. Opening his eyes, he saw reflected in the mirror above the bed that there was a deep depression on the mattress next to him, but no one was there!

There are also sightings of a little girl, and sometimes near the bar patrons hear a child crying or laughing. On one occasion very late at night, Tony saw a little girl run down the hall and go downstairs. She was wearing what looked to be an old fashioned dress, "like a Little House on the Prairie dress," as Tony described it. As strange as her clothing was, she looked so real that his initial reaction was that of annoyance.

"I thought who would be stupid enough to bring their little girl to a bar at this hour. I asked everyone whose kid it was, but no one spoke up. I went downstairs to get her, and couldn't find her anywhere. And no one saw her come back upstairs. She simply vanished."

Others, like Andre, have felt a tugging on their shirt or jacket, like a little child trying to get attention. But who could this little girl be? About twenty-five years ago when a house was being built nearby, a bulldozer unearthed a tombstone with the name of Elizabeth J. Smalley, the daughter of James Smalley, who died in the mid-1800s when she was only seven. The man who uncovered the stone (and most likely also disturbed her grave?) gave it to Tony's father, who stored it under the stairs in the basement. Did the stone also bring along the restless spirit of young Elizabeth Smalley?

Tony wanted to have some renovations done in the basement, so he hired a man to remove one of the original brick pillars, which was right by the basement stairs where the tombstone was kept. After working for just a short time, the man quit because he claimed that someone kept pushing him into the pile of bricks. Another man was hired, but he quit after claiming that as he worked someone kept pulling on his shirt. Finally, a third man was hired. He simply ran out, saying he just couldn't work down there. In fact, he left so suddenly that he didn't even take his tools—and he has refused to come back to Smalley's to get them! When little children want attention, they will do almost anything to get it, especially if they are dead.

The brick column and pile where several men refused to work.

After resting in the basement for twenty-five years, the tombstone was brought upstairs to be part of the spectacular Halloween display Tony puts up in the restaurant every year. He placed the stone near the long mirror (which also appears to have some paranormal properties) in the front dining room, and a patron asked Tony about it. She was a member of the Smalley family and was trying to construct a family tree. She very much wanted to have little Elizabeth's tombstone returned to her family. Tony was happy to oblige, but unfortunately, while the stone left the premises, the spirit of the little girl seems to have remained.

Perhaps one of Elizabeth's most recent pranks occurred just a few weeks before our visit. A busboy went downstairs to get something from the meat locker. The locker has an old style door with a heavy metal bar to hold it closed. When the bar is lifted, it falls over into a resting position where it is incapable of locking accidentally. The busboy opened the door, stepped inside the cold room, and the door suddenly slammed shut. Then somehow the bar rose up and over into the lock. He yelled for help and pounded on the door for over twenty terrifying minutes. Finally, someone noticed he was missing and a subsequent search found the shivering busboy locked inside the meat locker.

When our group entered Smalley's, Tony gave us a quick tour of the dining rooms and bar, all of which were decorated with marvelous life-sized Halloween witches and ghouls. It may come as no surprise that Halloween has always been one of my favorite holidays, and I was impressed—and a little envious—by these great decorations. Of course, I had to make a mental note of where all the fake skeletons and ghosts were on the walls, so I wouldn't be confused when my pictures were developed!

We were not inside more than a minute when the pay phone rang in the bar. Tony answered it, and he let me hear the strange static. This was not the steady hiss of static from a disconnected line—there were pauses and different types of sounds, almost as if someone was trying to talk over a very bad connection. Throughout the several hours of the ensuing investigation, that pay phone rang numerous times, and each time there was the same mysterious static.

It took me a few minutes to get all my equipment ready, and then we headed straight for the basement. Since I had the meters and the infrared camcorder that could see in the dark, I led the conga line of the curious into the depths of the old haunted inn. I really didn't expect much to happen with so many people there, but I quickly learned that the ghosts of Smalley's are not shy.

Almost immediately after we were all in the basement—standing near the base of the stairs where the tombstone was once kept, and where the pillar and pile of bricks stood—my EMF meter showed strong signs of activity. Then there were clear, loud footsteps creaking on the floorboards directly over our heads, moving toward the top of the staircase we had just descended. They were the loudest and most distinct footsteps I had ever heard. There was also something else that I had never heard before on an investigation—screaming. Since I have been doing this for many years in dozens of haunted locations, I forget that most people are scared senseless when they encounter the other world. Some of the members of our group were understandably nervous about coming to Smalley's, and disembodied footsteps over their heads was more than enough to cause them to verbally vent some of their fear.

Undeterred by the screams, or perhaps encouraged by them, our upstairs visitor continued all the way to the door at the top of the stairs. There he stopped—keeping us waiting breathlessly to see if he would continue down the stairs and head straight for us (I say he, because the footsteps sounded like heavy, male footsteps, perhaps in boots). It was one hell of a dramatic way to announce his presence, and I certainly shifted my attitude from a fun, casual tour for the radio station to a full alert, serious ghost investigation. If the spirits wanted my complete attention, they now had it.

The basement stairs.

When the footsteps stopped,

17

our group moved slowly and cautiously in the darkness back toward the liquor room. By this point Andre was on the phone with Woodman back in the studio, and they were live on the air. Perhaps the spirits sensed that, for they were ready to put on a good show. As we approached the small room with the bolted door, there were strange sounds emanating from within, and they were loud enough for everyone to hear. It was at this point that Tony mentioned that the room might have been used as a morgue when James Smalley was the coroner. Given the circumstances, it was not the most comforting news, learning that the noisy room before us once held bodies.

The door to the frightening liquor room.

However, we all continued to move forward, and when I reached the room I pulled up the metal bar and gave the door a tug. Cold air rushed out—at least ten degrees colder than the rest of the basement as measured by the thermometer—and EMF readings were high. Liquor bottles lined the shelves on either side of the tiny, low-ceilinged room, and the narrow space between shelves was only about two feet wide.

Over the phone, Woodman instructed Brook, who had been strongly effected by his first visit to Smalley's, to ask the spirits to come out and play. Brook started yelling, and more strange sounds caused more people to start screaming. It was clear I was with one terrified bunch of people! I thought it best to move away from the intimidating liquor room, so I closed and latched the door and the line of people turned around and headed away. However, we had not gone more than a few feet when some loud pounding noise began inside the supposedly empty liquor room. Our attention, apparently, was once again required.

I opened the door again and five of us crammed ourselves into the small space. I was the first in and my back was literally against the wall. It grew unnaturally cold in there, the EMF meter was registering a high field, and my skin was crawling. Whatever presence was with us, was very potent. Although I didn't feel frightened or threatened, I did start to feel a little dizzy and lightheaded. In rare instances, I get that feeling when confronted by a very strong presence. This was clearly one of those instances.

I suggested that Andre switch places with me to see if he had the same intense feeling I was experiencing. He hesitatingly moved to put his back against the wall, but that lasted less than five seconds.

"I don't like it," he declared moving away from the wall and out of the room. That was certainly putting it mildly.

The cold air, EMF readings and intense feeling slowly faded, and then I heard yelling back out in the open section of the basement. I exited the liquor room, securely closing the door behind me, and was told that more noises were being heard out in the darkness around them. The action had shifted from the liquor room to the other side of the basement. A good ghost hunter always follows the trail, so we all moved with the sounds, encountering more cold spots and high EMF readings.

19

The cramped interior of the liquor room.

Shortly after, we decided to investigate the meat locker where the busboy had been trapped. I opened the door, and tried to take a step forward, but was jerked to a stop. Someone had a hold of my coat and I couldn't move.

For god's sake, I thought, more than a bit exasperated, *I know these people are scared, but they're all adults. Did someone really have to grab hold of my coat like a little kid?*

In a way, I couldn't have been more right, although I didn't know it at that moment.

I asked who was holding me, and everyone replied that no one was even touching me. I then thought that my coat must have gotten caught on some type of hook, but in the darkness I ran my hand up and down the smooth wood frame and found that not a single hook or latch was there. There was simply nothing on which to get caught.

Then I decided I had better take a step back, and I was suddenly released from whatever had gripped me. Sandy Tomcho, one of the reporters from the *Times Herald Record*, was directly behind me, and she said that even though it was very dimly lit, she had clearly seen my coat sticking out straight behind me, but she couldn't see anything holding onto it! Tony turned on the lights, and we could not find any reason for my coat to have refused to follow me into the meat locker.

Just a few days earlier, I had given a lecture and someone asked if I had ever been physically grabbed by an entity, and I had said no. That night after visiting Smalley's, I had another lecture and was asked the same question. This time I couldn't say no.

Could I have gotten caught on something I couldn't see in the darkness? Of course, that would be the normal explanation. But if we sidestep the normal for a moment and look at the paranormal aspects, could little Elizabeth, or one of the other permanent residences of Smalley's, have been up to her old tricks of tugging on clothing for attention? It sure seemed to be the case.

As startling as this "death grip" was, I didn't have time to ponder its implications. We moved back to the infamous basement staircase, and weren't disappointed. Those very heavy footsteps passed directly overhead once again. I can't emphasize enough how clear they were. It wasn't as if there was some vague creaking of floorboards somewhere—these were unmistakable footsteps directly on the floor above us. No questions, no doubts.

This time, however, we had an extra bonus—whoever it was, walked right to a door near the top of the stairs and pounded on something. Tony knew exactly what it was, a massive lion head

21

knocker that hung there. Again, there was no mistaking the metallic banging sound of the knocker on that wooden door. These were such amazing phenomena I almost asked someone to pinch me to see if I was dreaming, but I quickly decided I had enough physical contact for the day.

The doors to the basement are black iron gates with blankets hung behind them, therefore there should not be any bright reflections.

Not surprisingly, there was a lot of fear in the group, and some people decided to give up the ghost hunt and go outside. For anyone who wants to visit a haunted place because they think it will be like some entertaining movie, think again. It's real, it's in your face, and you are on *their* territory. I've come across a lot of people who quickly change their minds, or have them changed for them, when they have their first real taste of an aggressive or demonstrative ghost.

Once again, the footsteps stopped at the top of the stairs. Nothing came down the stairs, and we didn't hear anything walk away. We waited, but there was only silence. Whatever it was, had disappeared on the spot.

There was yet another room in the basement, to the right of the stairs. This was a large room used for storage, and we had examined it earlier. When we went back in a second time, there was a horrible stench that had not been there previously. On the air, Brook told Woodman about it, emphasizing that it "smelled like something deceased" and it was so strong "that you have to hold your nose." There were high EMF readings again, but as they faded, so did the smell.

By this point, poor Brook was getting the feeling that the entities were attaching themselves to him, and he was getting rather upset. While everyone tried to soothe what seemed to be his unfounded fears, I was finding that there were very high EMF readings just around him, wherever he went. I even asked if he had a pacemaker or any other type of electrical device that might account for the readings. It was a phenomena I had never seen before, and I began to think he had every reason to be upset.

We left that room and returned to the staircase, and Woodman asked Andre to sit on the center of the stairs. I had recorded in infrared some white darting lights there, and due to all the footsteps we had previously heard on the floor above, it seemed to be a focal point of activity. Andre sat down, and I directed the camcorder at him. After just a few moments there were more footsteps, another knocking sound and then the door at the top of the stairs opened by itself! Andre literally jumped off the stairs. We checked to make sure no one was upstairs, and indeed, everyone not with us in the basement was outside. Everyone living, that is.

Woodman then suggested we check the liquor room again, and as we approached I was startled to see its door standing wide open! Several people had witnessed me close and secure the door, and like the bar on the meat locker, there was no way for it to move on its own. We entered the tight space again, and this time there was a sound like scraping glass, just inches from my head. We all heard it, and Brook became so terrified he was absolutely frozen with fear. His limbs were stiff and he couldn't move. Finally, he calmed down enough for us to leave the cold cramped room, but his belief that the spirits were in him was now stronger than ever. I was concerned that he might be right, and that he just might take a few home with him.

Fortunately, as the sun rose higher in the sky, the intense activity in Smalley's began to diminish. The ice-cold liquor room suddenly felt warm and the high EMF readings were gone. There were no more footsteps or pounding. Woodman and Andre did their best to convince Brook that he would not be taking any ghosts home, and when the high EMF readings around him were back to zero, he finally felt like the spirits' grip had been broken. The intense, terrifying, wild hours of bizarre activity seemed to be over. It was like some paranormal switch had been turned off and Smalley's basement seemed to be just like a normal basement, and its dining rooms and bar were not unlike those in any other restaurant.

I was relieved. I was relieved because the investigation had been mentally, emotionally and physically draining, and I was exhausted. It was so intense for so many hours that I was glad it was over. As I was driving home, I knew I would have to go back to Smalley's someday for another investigation, but that wouldn't be for quite a while. Or so I thought.

The next day I got a message from a reporter at a television station in Westchester County, NY. He had heard about Smalley's and wanted me to join him there very early the next morning to tape a show. I called him back fully intending to just say no, but he was both persistent and insistent, and I finally relented. I asked Mike Worden to join me, and once again I found myself at Smalley's at the crack of dawn.

The spirits weren't nearly as tired as I was, because they began their fun and games right away. Within minutes of our arriving, the infamous payphone in the bar started ringing. The reporter and his cameraman raced to the phone. Lifting the receiver, there was that same bizarre static. The cameraman placed his microphone near the earpiece and actually recorded the strange sounds. If either the reporter or the cameraman had been skeptical, they weren't any longer.

I contacted someone in the telephone company to discuss these unusual calls, and he determined that they were not calls made from any outside phones. In short, the payphone was inexplicably ringing on its own, and the static sounds were also of undetermined origin.

Perhaps not coincidentally, the payphone is directly across from the area of the bar where Brook had been physically pinned down, and Andre had been grabbed. Is some entity stuck at that particular area, trying to get the attention of anyone who steps inside his little world?

We continued re-examining all the hot spots, or cold spots, as the case may be, throughout Smalley's. The payphone rang on a few more occasions, and there were a few brief readings and strange sounds, but nothing at the level of the last investigation. Two factors may have been responsible.

First, it was later in the morning, when activity does seem to diminish. Second, there wasn't a large group of screaming, terrified people. That energy of fear may just have fed the activity during the previous investigation. Still, it was far from being normal, and what we did encounter only reaffirmed what we already believed—the Smalley Inn is haunted upstairs and down.

I called Tony Porta several months later to see what had been transpiring. He said that since our last visit, things had been remarkably quiet. There had clearly been some kind of shift, to the point where employees didn't actually feel frightened going into the basement, or being alone in other sections of the place. He was reluctant to have us return for a further investigation, for fear of stirring everything up again.

Let sleeping ghosts lie. I couldn't agree more.

While I doubt that every spirit that inhabited the old inn has gone, perhaps all the attention has somehow soothed their troubled souls. For decades, and maybe even centuries, these entities may simply have been waiting for the opportunity to let the world of the living know that they still existed. Hopefully, some have found peace.

There is also the possibility that all of the mischievous spirits are gathering their energy for the next Halloween season, when they will once again lock people in rooms, grab patrons by the bar, and allow fleeting glimpses of their ethereal forms.

There's only one way to find out for sure. Go to the Smalley Inn late one night, and find out for yourself.

Seven O'clock Shadow

In 1994, sixteen-year-old Patrick began helping his cousin renovate a house in the small hamlet of Edenville, New York. The structure was built in the 1800s, and the project was designed to convert the two-family house into a one-family, and restore both the interior and exterior to its original style.

Every day after work, Patrick would meet his cousin at the house and they would spend several hours working. One summer's evening around 7pm as they were finishing up, Patrick's cousin asked him to go upstairs and turn off the fluorescent work lights. Previously, there had been two staircases leading up to the second floor bedrooms, but one had been removed as part of the one-family conversion plan.

The remaining staircase led up to the right side of the long U-shaped second story, with two bedrooms being to the right of the landing, a bathroom about in the middle of the curve, and the master bedroom on the left tip of the unusual floor plan. As Patrick climbed the stairs, he wasn't thinking about anything other than the work they had accomplished that night. He had no trepidation about going upstairs alone, as he had done countless times before. There was nothing spooky or unusual about the house, and he never even considered that there was anything out of the ordinary there. However, that was all to change in one terrifying heartbeat.

About half way up the stairs, he looked up to the landing and saw something run from the bedroom area on the right, across the landing and into the bathroom. It was a dark, shadowy figure, but there was just enough detail to get the impression that it was a short, old man. An icy chill shot through Patrick's body, and in a state of near panic, he ran back downstairs to get his cousin, who was in the bathroom with the door closed—but this was no time for modesty.

Shoving open the door, Patrick shouted, "I saw something upstairs! I don't know what it was, but I saw something!"

He insisted that his cousin immediately follow him, and as they hurried to the staircase, Patrick tried to explain what he just saw. It wasn't easy. But then, they say a picture is worth a thousand words.

As they neared the second floor landing, Patrick was pointing out the route that the shadowy little figure had taken. He swung around to point to where the man ended his short sprint, and there was the dark image standing half in and half out of the bathroom.

"There he is!" Patrick yelled, as his cousin wheeled around just in time to glimpse the terrifying human-like shape pull itself quickly back into the darkness of the bathroom—and vanish.

From that day, Patrick was so scared that he refused to be in the house after 7pm, the time when strange things continued to happen. He also refused to ever be in the house alone, regardless of the time. If his cousin had to run out for supplies, he would sit out on the porch and wait for him to return. These may have been drastic measures, considering that the figure did not appear to be threatening, but Patrick wasn't the only one who didn't want to be in that house.

One the masons who worked with his cousin also happened to train seeing-eye dogs. These dogs are true wonders of the canine world, tirelessly following their master's commands with precision and courage. However, when the mason came by one evening to do some work, he brought one of the dogs, and this dog absolutely refused to step foot inside the house. Several times the man commanded the dog to go in, but the agitated dog steadfastly refused—something he had never done before. This inexplicable episode did not end at the doorstep, either, as for several days after, the dog's behavior was still noticeably out of character. Obviously, something had terrified the poor animal out of his very keen senses.

As strange occurrences continued, most of which happened at the same time in the evening, they began to refer to their punctual entity as their Seven O'clock Shadow. It was a good way to relieve some of the tension of the situation, but simply making light of the dark figure didn't make it go away.

On another occasion, his cousin's wife came to the house, opened the front door and said, "Hello." A male voice from upstairs returned the greeting with a loud and clear, "Hello." Naturally assuming it was her husband, the woman went upstairs, but after searching every room, found no sign of him. She then looked out the window and saw that her husband was hard at work in the backyard, so it would have been completely impossible for him to be the one who greeted her. Since her

28

husband was outside and the upstairs was empty, she realized it had to have been a disembodied male voice welcoming her.

That was the last straw. There was no way they were going to move into such a house with their children. They asked their priest to perform a blessing, and fortunately, it seemed to work. After the religious ceremony was completed, there were no more sightings of dark figures darting around hallways, no voices coming out of thin air, and nothing more to indicate that this little old man was still in residence.

Of course, as is always the question in such cases, was there anything in the history of this place to substantiate the claims that an old man was haunting that Edenville home? Unfortunately, in most cases there are usually no records or evidence available. However, in this instance, the evidence was openly disclosed by the sellers—although Patrick's cousin had no idea at the time.

Due to the famous legal battle over the haunted house on LaVeta Place in Nyack, New York, in the early 1990s (see the story in *Ghost Investigator, Volume 1*), laws had been passed around the country stating that owners who believed their property was haunted, were obligated to disclose the paranormal information to potential buyers. Failure to do so could render the contract null and void, and any money offered as a down payment would be returned.

Apparently, the previous owners cleverly decided to disclose their ghost in a manner that appeared to be a joke, yet legally satisfied their obligation. Out of the blue, one of the owners said with a laugh, "And if you see anyone running around the house, don't worry, it's just our grandfather."

What seemed to be amusing at the time, quickly lost its humorous aspect the moment the ghost of the old man rushed out of the darkness in front of a sixteen-year-old boy. Almost a decade has now passed since that terrifying day, but Patrick can still recall every second in vivid detail. Although there have been no further occurrences, you can be assured that when darkness begins to fall in Edenville, those who encountered the phantom grandfather will be looking over their shoulders to see if the Seven O'clock Shadow has returned.

***

In an interesting side note, when Patrick's cousin was excavating in the backyard, he uncovered a nineteenth century gravestone. The inscription revealed that the deceased had left this earth in 1877, on the 7th day of the 7th month.

Perhaps the number seven isn't so lucky at this house.

Homespun Farm

If you prefer to spend the night with kinder, gentler spirits, then look no further than Homespun Farm Bed and Breakfast in Griswold, Connecticut. Equally comforting for guests, that description can also be applied to the owners, Kate and Ron Bauer, who lovingly restored and preserved the house after years of neglect. While they endured long, hard hours of work, at times they received some friendly help from former residents—rather unique help considering the fact that these residents were no longer alive.

The main house was constructed in 1740 by Simon Brewster, the great-great grandson of William Brewster. William, who came over on the Mayflower in 1620, was instrumental in the founding of Plymouth Colony. Generations of Brewsters continued to occupy the house for the next 250 years, becoming locally renowned for their dairy farm and fruit orchards. When the family finally decided to get out of the farming business in 1991, the house and its 252 acres were sold to a developer.

A nineteenth century view of the house.

The house today.

The majority of the old orchard, which contained row upon row of apple and pear trees, was cut down and converted into a golf course. Fortunately, the house was not demolished, but it did lay vacant for five years. Actually, it wasn't technically vacant, as all manner of rodents had taken up comfortable lodgings inside. Then there were those former residents, who may have been waiting patiently in the cold, dark shadows for someone to come along and bring life back to the once-thriving homestead.

For those who believe that there is no such thing as fate, that there is only coincidence, consider the story of how the Bauers came to own the place. In 1995, they were staying at a bed and breakfast in the Griswold area, and they mentioned to the owner how much they loved old houses. The owner told them that the Brewster house was for sale, and they took a drive to see it. Despite its forlorn and overgrown appearance, they both felt that this might be the place of their dreams, although at that time it seemed to be a financial impossibility. However, over the following months, they found themselves driving by again and again. One day, they finally decided to stop and take a closer look. Concealed in an overgrown hedge, they uncovered the realtor's sign and gave her a call.

Unfortunately, wild shrubbery would be the least of their obstacles. For starters, Ron was in the Navy, and he was scheduled to be deployed in a submarine headed for the North Pole, so time was at a premium. Arranging a showing with the realtor proved difficult, but finally they met on the doorstep of the Brewster house in early spring, anxious to see the inside of this grand old home. The realtor placed the key in the lock, but it wouldn't turn. She applied greater pressure—to the point where the key was actually bending—but still the lock wouldn't budge. The realtor told Kate and Ron that they would have to reschedule for another time, as she would need to bring someone out to the house to resolve the problem. Kate informed the woman that since Ron was leaving in just two weeks, it had to be now or never. She asked for the key to give it a try, but the realtor was afraid that it would break off in the lock.

"I told her that I would pay for a locksmith if I broke the key," Kate recalled in the cozy nook off the kitchen, near the stubborn door that wouldn't yield to the realtor. "She reluctantly handed me the key, I put it in the lock, and it turned as smoothly as butter, opening the door to this home for us."

As they entered, the Bauers immediately felt a warm, comforting feeling, as if they had "always lived there"—despite all the decay and debris. The floors were littered with acorns and chestnuts from the years of animal habitation. Paint was peeling off the ceiling, and sheets of yellowed wallpaper had come unglued. In short, it was a complete mess, but they were able to see beneath the dirt to what the house had been, and what it could be again.

While Ron went off to sea, Kate handled the process of selling their house, buying the Brewster house and moving their belongings and three sons in early August of 1998. The three boys were considerably less than thrilled about leaving their friends and moving into what they saw as only a run down old house. The situation didn't improve, either, when they discovered that there was no hot water, and the toilet didn't flush. However, after spending the first night in the house, what had threatened to be a fraternal mutiny turned around one hundred and eighty degrees. Something had captivated the boys. In fact, while eating breakfast at a picnic table in the kitchen on the second morning after moving in, her thirteen-year-old, Jacob, suddenly looked at her and said thoughtfully, "Mom, there have been a lot of kids raised in this house."

"He wasn't asking me, he was telling me," Kate recalled. "And I just looked at him and thought how strange it was for a boy his age to think of such a thing. We weren't even talking about the house or anything like that. So I just told him that yes, there had a lot of kids brought up in this house. He just had that feeling, which was really neat.

That's when I took him around and showed him the thresholds and how worn out they are, and showed him the dips in the stairs from all the little feet that have gone up and down them. It was just nice that the energy of the house gave him that feeling, as horrible as it looked in the beginning."

Once the major issues of getting settled in the house had been addressed, and the kids had started school, Kate had some time for the property. There were several forty-five-foot long rows of blueberry bushes that were at the end of their season for producing fruit. Ron would be returning from sea in a couple of weeks, but Kate knew the berries would be long gone by that time, and she wanted to be able to at least save a handful of blueberries in the freezer for him. However, before she could pick a single berry off the bushes, she had to be able to get to them. The years of neglect had engulfed the bushes in tangles of poison ivy and brambles, so Kate set about clearing all the unwanted vegetation—a job that took several days of hard work.

Once she was able to reach the bushes, she decided they needed some pruning. Although Kate had completed a course of study to become a Master Gardener, she had never specifically pruned blueberry bushes, so she just began cutting as she thought best. However, she quickly had the feeling that she was not alone in her task.

"I felt like someone was watching me, and I kept looking behind me but no one was there. And then I thought I was just being silly because I was alone in a new place, with no neighbors. But the longer I worked, the more I felt that not only was someone watching me, but telling me how to prune. There were no words, it was more of a feeling when I would reach for a certain branch and I could almost hear, 'No, not that one,' or 'Yes, that one.' I really got into the flow of work and two hours passed before I knew it."

34

The blueberry bushes.

Even though Kate never heard actual words, she did feel a very strong presence. Several times she thought she saw a distinctive figure out of the corner of her eye—a tall, thin man in overalls—but each time the image eluded her when she turned to get a better look. As bizarre as it sounded, Kate had to conclude that it felt as though someone was there to guide her in taking care of the bushes.

"When Ron came home, I didn't tell him what had happened, because I was afraid he would think I was just being paranoid. But then in November, after we had finally cleared our way to the orchard on our property, Ron started pruning the old fruit trees.

I was inside making supper, and he came in just after dark and sat down to take his boots off and said, 'I had the weirdest feeling when I was out in the orchard.'

That just gave me goose bumps and I said, really, what do you mean?

And he said, 'Well, I was pruning, and it was like someone was telling me how to prune.'

So I asked if he had heard voices, and he said there wasn't a voice, but he felt that a tall man in overalls was standing there directing him!

That's when I finally told him my story, and it was the exact same thing. I hadn't mentioned a word about the man in overalls telling me how to prune the blueberries, and here was Ron having the same experience. From then on it happened all the time. Whenever we are outside working hard we feel his presence."

This has led to a very unique method of ghost hunting. People who have heard about the spirits of Homespun Farm want to know how and where they can encounter them, perhaps expecting that a séance at midnight might do the trick.

"I just tell them to grab a pair of pruning shears and go outside and do some work," Kate said smiling. She did not elaborate on how many surprised guests actually took her up on the suggestion.

With such a long history, spanning many generations and two and a half centuries, could there be any hope in identifying this phantom gardener? Remarkably, yes. A member of the Brewster family stopped by one day with some old pictures of the farm and some family members. Among them, was a face and figure Kate immediately recognized—a tall, gaunt man with distinctive features.

The mysterious man in overalls, whom she and Ron had so frequently encountered, was Simon Brewster—not the one who had built the house in 1740—but his descendant who owned the farm for much of the twentieth century, until his death in the 1970s. It was a stunning discovery, finally coming face to face with the old farmer who had been "telling" them how to prune his beloved trees and bushes. As the last male of the long Brewster line to manage the lands, perhaps he still feels an obligation to make sure they continue to be taken care of properly—a bond between man and earth that not even death could break.

So, as Simon Brewster keeps a watchful eye on things outside, is anyone patrolling the inside of the house? Even if one discounts the subtle energy of the place that makes you feel at home and turns your thoughts to generations gone by, there are some more obvious signs that other Brewsters are still about.

Perhaps the most obvious examples of this are the many times that Kate has heard a woman in the kitchen calling her name, only to find that she is alone in the house. Unlike the silent Simon who only says things in thoughts, this voice is loud and clear and perfectly audible. There never seems to be any urgency or distress in the voice as her name is being called, just a simple summons for her attendance, or perhaps a gracious acknowledgement by a former lady of the house to the present owner. In any case, it is never frightening, just another interesting example of the link between past and present at Homespun Farm.

Simon and Laura Brewster

There are other signs that, while the men folk tend to the outside, the ladies watch over the house. One night when their son Jacob was alone, he heard a woman's footsteps coming up the back staircase to the second floor. The footsteps continued into the hallway, paused near his bedroom door, and then continued down the front staircase. Knowing that he was supposed to be alone, he grabbed his Boy Scout knife and kept still. When nothing more happened, he realized it was most likely not a living woman who had made those sounds.

Surprisingly, once he got over the initial shock, he found that he wasn't really scared. In fact, the next morning after describing the incident, he told Kate that it actually reminded him of her footsteps when she came to check on him each night at bedtime. So, perhaps, when Kate was not there, someone else took it upon herself to make sure the boy was all right.

While it was tempting to think that this occurrence was merely old creaking floorboards or the product of a boy's imagination, it became harder to discount when it occurred again and again, whenever Jacob was alone at night. The pattern was always the same—a woman's footsteps climbing the back stairs, a pause, then the footsteps fading away down the front staircase. But then it really got strange...

"I started finding bobby pins at the base of the staircase," Kate explained. "I had long hair at the time, but I never used any kind of hairpins, especially the old-fashioned kind like I kept finding. And I don't know how to put this any other way, but I am a compulsive vacuumer, and there's no way these things could have been laying around the floor for any length of time without me finding them."

Whenever one appeared, usually following a night of the phantom footsteps, Kate would pick it up and put it in the special display cabinet which held all of the artifacts they had discovered while working on the house and grounds. There were bits of pottery, an old doll's dress, tools and other bits and pieces of families long gone. The hairpins, of course, were the most unique items on display, as they seemed to have materialized out of thin air.

However, the tale of the puzzling hairpins does not end there. Even though the footsteps ended when Jacob moved out, and the hairpins subsequently stopped appearing, no one thought that they might then begin disappearing. During my investigation, I asked Kate if I could photograph some of them. She obligingly opened the cabinet to get out a few, but didn't see any. She got a flashlight and carefully searched through every bit and piece in the cabinet, but couldn't find a single one. It seemed as if these hairpins had all returned to thin air!

Contents of the cabinet—minus the hairpins.

As incredible as it might seem for small pins to appear, such occurrences pale in comparison to what showed up on the property one moonlit night. There are still Brewster family members who occasionally stop by to reminisce about the old farm, and one of Simon's nieces came to spend the night in 2001. It was a wonderful opportunity for Kate to learn more of the history of the house and its people, and the niece was thrilled to be able to recall happy childhood memories from decades ago. However, while it is always exciting to see things from one's past, it's usually better if these things really exist.

It was about two or three in the morning when Simon's niece awoke and was unable to get back to sleep. It was a warm night with a beautiful full moon, so she decided to go outside and sit in the garden for a while. She was facing south, looking across the little road that separated the main house from the barn complex. There was a green barn directly across the street, but her gaze fell upon the larger, more impressive red barn behind it. The bright moonlight displayed the old barn in vivid detail, and she thought of all the enjoyable times she had spent there. After about an hour, she went back inside and was finally able to get back to sleep.

Mid-twentieth century aerial view of the Brewster farm. The orchards at the top half of the photo are now a golf course. The red barn forms the left arm of the U-shaped barn complex.

At breakfast, she told Kate more stories about the farm, and mentioned how beautiful the old barn looked in the moonlight. As the green barn was not the most attractive structure, Kate asked something to the effect of, "Really? You think the green barn still looks good?"

The niece looked puzzled and replied, "No, I mean the red barn, of course."

Kate was stunned for moment, and then asked the woman to repeat what she had said. Her story was the same. She awoke in the middle of the night, went outside and sat in the garden and looked at the red barn, which she could clearly see in the moonlight.

Nice story. One problem. The red barn was no longer standing. It had been completely demolished several years earlier. The niece could not believe it, and had to look again in the daylight to be convinced.

While this may conjure up many old expressions about the broad side of a barn, this is one sighting that can not be dismissed as fog, reflections, swamp gas or any other explanations generally offered up by skeptics. It's close to impossible to mistake anything else for an entire barn.

View of the green barn. The larger red barn used to stand behind it.

There have been several less dramatic, but no less inexplicable, stories from guests. In the Orchard Room downstairs, a woman was in bed with her husband one night when the light suddenly came on. Her husband was sound asleep, the door was closed, and no one else was in the room. And it certainly was not possible for her to accidentally turn it on herself, as the light is operated by a pull cord by the door, which is at least ten feet away from where she was on the bed.

Pear Room guests have their share of reports, specifically of footsteps leading up the short staircase from the kitchen. These footsteps are generally heard late at night, or very early in the morning.

The Pear Room was once occupied by Frank, an old farmhand who died in the 1950s. It's not known if he died on the farm, but perhaps those early morning footsteps are just the phantom sounds of work boots heading out for another day's labor.

The Pear Room staircase. There are a few orbs in this photo I took. After Kate saw it, she said she had always had trouble photographing this room because of white spots of light that appeared, which she assumed was a problem with the camera or film, even though the spots only appeared in this room.

The Bauer's adorable Yorkie-Chihuahua mix, Whimsy, has also taken notice of things that apparently only she can see and hear. She will stare intently, or jump with a start when there is no movement or sounds to be sensed by the human occupants of the house. Whimsy is not a nervous, high-strung dog, so when she acts this way, Kate takes notice.

Whimsy cuddles up on a pillow in the front room off the kitchen.

While it is fascinating to hear such stories, there is definitely no substitute for being there, so on March 18, 2003, fellow ghost investigator Mike Worden and I visited Homespun Farm Bed and Breakfast. When first glimpsing the house and surrounding property, the immediate sense is that this is a place filled with history. I could also appreciate that the orchards across the street became a golf course with rolling green lawns, rather than a huge shopping center as was once proposed. Now that would have been frightening!

After lugging in our bags of gear, I interviewed Kate about her experiences at Homespun Farm. One of the first things I learned was that the place earned its name by the fact that she and her husband had

43

done all the work on the house themselves—even to the extent that Ron made beautiful beds from rich oak boards salvaged from buildings on the farm. As I had recently completed an exhausting project involving the removal of stubborn wallpaper from one room in my own house, I was suitably impressed by both the incredible quantity and quality of work the Bauers had done restoring this large colonial gem. I will never again complain about any of my small home projects. (Well, I'll probably still complain, but just not quite as much.)

Mike and I decided to get some dinner while waiting for darkness to fall to begin our investigation. We were going to head down to Mystic, Connecticut, which is only about fifteen minutes from Griswold, but we first came upon Foxwoods casino. That was as far as we got. From the time I learned to play poker as a pre-schooler (that's another story), I have always had a soft spot for a friendly wager. In any event, it was interesting to see the obsessive characters who cling to the slot machines and flock around the craps tables, chain smoking and drinking, unable to break free of their compulsive behaviors—prime candidates for future ghosts of America!

When we returned to the farm, the sun had set and a bright full moon was casting just the right shadows to set the mood for a ghost hunt. The spring thaw had made the ground spongy, and the gurgling sounds emanating from the soft earth all around us added a nice eerie touch. We began out by the blueberry bushes. The digital cameras picked up some very bright orbs, but nothing in infrared or with the EMF meters. There was a noise from one of the nearby garages—something like two pieces of metal banging together—but the sound did not repeat and we had no way of knowing its source. It caught our attention, though, as did the cow's abrupt and loud mooing when our backs were turned.

We continued to scan and photograph the property, and found that the only other spot that had pronounced anomalies was the garden by the house. The next morning Kate told us that was the area where the old slave quarters once stood. It was certainly news to us, as we had no idea that the Brewsters had owned slaves.

When we were finished outside, we were more than happy to escape the damp, chilly night air and to go back inside the warm, cozy house. Our first objective was the Orchard Room, where one guest had reported the light turning on by itself. As I began taking pictures with my digital camera, I took note of the fact that I had exactly 62 minutes of battery life left. It's something I habitually check on an investigation, as the last thing you want to do is to blow a night's work on dead batteries.

I took one picture of the bed, and then my camera went dead. My initial thought was that the camera had broken—after all, I knew for certain that I had an hour of battery time. Just to be sure, I went back upstairs for the spare battery, popped it in, and the camera sprang to life. It didn't make any sense, and once again I checked the first battery and it was completely drained. This was a first—I have had problems with electrical equipment in many haunted locations, but I had yet to come across anything that could instantly drain an hour's worth of power out of a battery. (I recharged it that night and it has worked flawlessly ever since.)

The Orchard Room

When we went back upstairs to the Pear Room, Mike found that his camcorder was off. Before we left, he had set up the camera on a tripod and began shooting in infrared to see if anything happened

45

while we were gone. Apparently, something did happen, because somehow the camcorder was switched off as we were leaving the room. This can only be done by manually pressing buttons, and we were on the other side of the room on the way out when it shut off.

A pattern was clearly developing. Nothing frightening or overly dramatic like slamming doors or misty apparitions, just unmistakable things to get our attention—and to possibly hinder *our* ability to gather too much evidence about *them*.

Then Mike decided to try to open a direct dialogue, so with infrared camcorders running, he asked if there was anyone who wanted to communicate. Immediately, a flurry of little darting lights moved past him. I couldn't see anything with my eyes, but they appeared clearly in infrared. We took the answer to Mike's question to be yes, but nothing else subsequently occurred—at that time.

While I had trouble sleeping in my room, although nothing unusual seemed to be happening, things were a lot more active in Mike's room. He explains:

"I had difficulty sleeping, most of which I attributed to the unfamiliar room and bed. When I first retired, there was an electric candle light in the window adjacent to the bed. It was close to my eyes, so I unscrewed the bulb by a good half turn or so to turn off the light. The first time I awoke after that, I immediately noticed that the light was lit again, and the bulb was firmly in place. I promptly unscrewed it again and attempted to sleep. I tossed and turned most of the night, sleeping for short periods of time, then awakening suddenly. Nothing really caused me to wake up, that I could tell, although a few times in the night I heard distinct foot steps and floor boards creaking from outside the door to my room."

Discovering the light bulb being screwed back in and the light on again was obviously a surprise, but it did not affect Mike as much as the visit he would have in the middle of the night.

"I don't consider myself to be psychic, however, I am sensitive to psychic phenomena. At about 3:30am or so, I awakened, and as I lay in the bed I had a very distinct impression of an older female presence, and this presence felt domineering and very strong willed. Almost as if the woman would have been seen as uncompromising, even overbearing. I did not have the impression of evil or negativity associated with this woman—rather it was more of what her personality was like in life. I think that this was the first time that I can recall ever having such a vivid impression."

Mike's room.

I didn't know anything about Mike's visitor until we were leaving. After breakfast (which was outrageously delicious French toast), Kate helped us carry our gear back to the car. As we walked, she talked about Simon's wife Laura, who had been suffering from Alzheimer's since the late 1980s (one of the reasons the farm was sold in 1991), and had recently died in January of 2003. Kate explained that Simon had been the most eligible bachelor of his time—single, well off, and in his late 40s—when Laura caught his eye. The locals never forgave the out-of-towner for finally snagging "their" best bachelor, and the fact that Laura was also of a different faith only made matters worse.

Although ostracized by the community, she continued to run the farm for years after Simon's death. In fact, as Kate put it, "Laura ruled the farm with an iron fist."

That rang a loud bell with Mike, and as we were driving away he described his strong-willed visitor. Could it have been Laura Brewster, accepting Mike's invitation to communicate and letting him know that she was still watching over *her* farm?

When I got home, I looked over my notes and reviewed the digital images and some of the video footage. Initially, I had come away from the investigation with the impression that there was not a lot of paranormal activity at Homespun Farm, but as I tallied up the inexplicable incidents and photographic evidence, I was puzzled as to why I was under that misconception. Then I realized that it was because, regardless of all that had happened, there was never any feeling of threats or danger. I guess after so many years of dealing with nasty, aggressive hauntings, when I encounter tranquil spirits they don't register with the same impact.

Now, as I review the case, it's evident that Homespun Farm Bed and Breakfast offers experiences on many different levels. Whether you like to soak in a claw foot tub with aromatherapy bubbles, stroll through the gardens and orchards, or drive ten minutes away for the country's largest casino, there's something of interest for everyone. And maybe, just maybe, you will experience something of the past—a friendly reminder from generations gone by of the love, caring and hard work that went into two and a half centuries of an American family.

At the very least, Kate and Ron Bauer will welcome you like family and make you feel at home. And you can look at those stairs and contemplate the people and circumstances that wore upon them, through good times and bad, through births, marriages and deaths. Even if the spirits are unwilling to talk, the house speaks volumes, and thanks to people like the Bauers, its story may continue for centuries to come.

Night Visitor

The names have been changed, the exact location
has not been revealed, and faces have been blurred
to protect the owner's privacy.

In 1997, Dan began work on a piece of land in Westtown, New York. It was part of an old orchard, and using natural fill from the site, a small pond was filled in and the ground was made level. In the months that followed, Dan built a spacious house, which he intended to use as a rental property. Nothing unusual occurred during construction, and there were no indications that the new home might have more occupants than he anticipated.

In February of 1998, the house was completed and the first tenants were his sister, Barbara, her husband, Bill, and their two-year-old daughter, Janice. The family quickly settled in and felt very comfortable with their new place. It wasn't until after Barbara's ten-year-old stepson, Derek, moved in at the end of the summer that some things began getting uncomfortable.

"It started with footsteps going up and down the hall," Barbara recalls. "They would go the entire length of the hall, but not any further than that. In addition to the footsteps, there was kind of a swishing sound, like corduroy pants legs rubbing together, or a nylon windbreaker type of outfit."

The footsteps would begin near the kitchen and travel down the hallway towards the bedrooms, stopping in front of Derek's room. There would be a pause, then a few more steps to Janice's room, where they would stop again. Although Barbara would repeatedly get up to see who was there, both children would be sound asleep and the rest of the house would be empty. The clear, distinct footsteps were terrifying, however Barbara didn't mention them to Bill, and she certainly didn't say anything to the children. But then, she didn't need to say anything to Janice, as their young daughter began to have her own conversations.

In the middle of the night, Janice would talk to her "friend"—a boy who she said would come to visit her at night to play. While it is not unusual for children to have imaginary playmates, when coupled with the footsteps that would come down the hall to her room before

49

she began talking, it appeared as if this was something more than a child's imagination. Janice never gave her friend a name, or indicated his age, but she was adamant about the fact that her male friend did exist, and continued to get up at night to talk to him.

If there was a "friend" in the house, he was not eager to be discovered. Barbara always slept with her back toward the bedroom door, but often she would turn over to try to see who was in the hall. Obviously aware of her movements, she would hear the invisible visitor retreating rapidly, or "scurrying away" as she described it.

Then there were the many nights when Barbara was sitting on the couch in the living room, and she saw someone walking down the hall and then turning into the kitchen. As it was dark, and her angle of vision was narrow, she could only see what she described as "a whitish figure." The first time, she thought it was Derek in his pajamas, and she called out his name. When there was no response, she went to investigate and found the kitchen empty, and Derek sound asleep. This happened repeatedly, yet still she didn't mention anything to her husband.

Finally, one night when they were in bed and the footsteps once again could be clearly heard coming down the hall, Bill asked, "Did you hear that?!"

"I said thank god he heard it, because I had been hearing it for months," Barbara said, expressing the relief that comes when you realize you are not the only one being confronted by the paranormal. "We finally talked about it and he told me that he had been hearing the same footsteps all along but didn't want to say

Looking down the hallway where the phantom footsteps are heard.

50

anything. He had also been seeing the white figure going into the kitchen."

They then asked Derek if he ever experienced anything unusual at night, and the boy said that he often heard someone walking in the hall, but always assumed it was one of them. Several times he followed the sounds of the footsteps into the kitchen, but no one was ever there.

They began to put some of the pieces of the puzzle together and found that the silent white figure that entered the kitchen always approached it from the same direction (the kitchen can be entered from the hallway or from the living room area), and it usually appeared before midnight. The footsteps usually occurred between 1:30am and 4am. Once they recognized what was happening, they tried a little experiment and kept the lights on all night. Whenever the lights were on, the visitor stayed away.

Only two things have happened during the day. On one occasion while Bill was vacuuming, he had the unnerving feeling that he was not alone. It was as if someone was standing directly behind him, and the feeling grew so intense that it actually felt as though someone was breathing on the back of his neck.

Another day, the family was preparing to go out shopping. Bill went into Janice's room to get her, and he saw that her room was a real mess, with toys and clothes covering the floor. As they left, Bill said that as soon as they got home she would have to clean her room. Many hours later when they returned to the empty house, they were stunned to find that everything that had been on Janice's floor had been picked up and piled onto the bed! Perhaps her friend was trying to help?

One of the most frightening events took place late one night. As they all slept, there was a deafening crashing sound in the kitchen.

"We thought the cabinets had all fallen off the wall and all the pots and pans had come out," Barbara explained, still visibly effected years later. "And you know that sound, like a pot lid spinning on the floor, you could hear that too. We both flew up out of bed and ran into the kitchen, but there wasn't a single thing out of place! We searched everywhere, and couldn't find any reason for that terrible crashing sound. And the kids were still asleep and never heard a thing."

Then there was an even more unusual, but possibly crucial, piece to the puzzle. One night when Bill was working, Barbara came home, opened the front door and was hit with the overwhelming odor of beer. The smell was everywhere, and given the fact that they didn't drink and never kept alcohol in the house, it was all the more disconcerting.

She searched the house and didn't find anyone, but the beer smell was so intense Barbara finally called the police. As she tried to explain the situation, she realized how crazy it sounded and told them to forget the whole thing. It was close to an hour before the strong beer odor finally faded.

After more than two years of living with the unwanted visitor and the bizarre events, Barbara and Bill purchased a new house and moved out. Much to their relief, the visitor did not follow them—no footsteps, no crashing sounds and no more late night conversations between their daughter and her friend. After having a chance to get settled and relax in their new home, Barbara realized just how stressful it had been living every day with the unknown. However, while she and her family were now beyond the reach of this restless spirit, the new tenants weren't so lucky.

Dan said that one day while talking with his new tenant—several months after he and his family had moved in—the man pointedly asked, "By the way, did you forget to tell us something about the house?" Dan asked what he meant, as he had never mentioned a word about ghosts to any of them. The man explained that he and his family kept hearing footsteps in the hall, and his young daughter had a male "friend" who visited her at night! There hadn't been any incidents terrifying enough to drive them away, but they just wanted their landlord to know that they, too, had encountered the night visitor.

In March of 2003, I spoke to Dan and arranged an investigation for a weekday evening. The house was vacant at the time, but new tenants were scheduled to move in that weekend, so time was of the essence.

A few days earlier, Barbara had asked Janice if she wanted to go back and visit the house, and the six-year-old began crying to the point of hysteria. As she was a happy child who rarely cried or got upset, this was a dramatic reaction. Despite the fact that Janice had claimed that this entity had been her friend at the time, it was now clear that she was terrified at the mere thought of returning. Perhaps more had occurred than their daughter had dared mention.

Bill and Barbara agreed not to bring Janice back to the house, but as the day approached she became insistent about going. It didn't make sense since she was initially so upset, but they finally relented.

Bob and I arrived at the Westtown house at 7pm, and Mike Worden and his sister, Melissa, and brother, Scott, were right behind us. There didn't appear to be anything unusual about the place from the outside—just a typical new house not unlike the many others that have sprung up across the former farmlands of Orange County. Barbara and Janice arrived a few minutes before Dan, so we had a chance to talk about some of the things that occurred in the house during those interesting two years.

I asked about the history of the land, and as far back as anyone could remember, that spot had been cultivated farmland with orchards and corn. I also asked if there had been any antiques brought into the house, or unusual old items that might possibly have some phantom strings attached, but that also seemed to be a dead end. As cars whizzed by on the road behind us, I suddenly had another thought—had there ever been any fatal accidents on this section of road?

Barbara then recalled that they had asked the local historian about the land where the house was built. The elderly woman told them about the people and their farms in the area, and then she mentioned something else. There had been a terrible accident many years ago. A young man was drunk and crashed his car near that spot. Whether unconscious or pinned in the wreck, the young man was unable to escape as the wrecked car caught fire and he died a horrible death.

Do you ever get that little tickle on the back of your neck, when you know something is ringing true? Well, I had that feeling tenfold. Not only did it feel right at the time, later when I began working on this story something else hit me. I kept thinking about Barbara's description of the terrible crashing sound she and Bill heard that one night, and how she specifically mentioned the distinct sound of something like pot lids spinning on the floor. As I wrote about it, I suddenly realized that there is something else that makes that sound—a metal hubcap that that is knocked loose after an accident and then spins on the pavement. I knew it was pure speculation, but it *felt* right.

So, what if we try to put the pieces of the puzzle together on the premise that an accident victim walks the halls of this Westtown house? The driver was a young man, and both Janice and the other young girl who lived in the house claimed that their friend was male. The man's death occurred late at night, when most of the paranormal events occur. Barbara encountered an overwhelming smell of beer, and the driver died as a result of being drunk. Finally, a crashing car would make a terrible sound like the one they heard in the kitchen, and the metal hubcaps of older cars would make that "pot lid" sound.

53

Had this young man, who had died so long ago, been waiting on the road where he died—waiting for someone with whom he could communicate and end his years of loneliness? When Dan built the house on the site and Barbara's family moved in, did this man also take up residence as a way of once again connecting with the world of the living, after he had so foolishly thrown away his own life?

It makes sense—as much as anything can under the circumstances—and it remained to be seen whether the night visitor would leave any measurable traces of himself in the house. Just minutes after Dan arrived and opened the front door, I took a picture of Barbara and Janice in the living room. (As there was no furniture in the place, we all sat on the floor.) There were several orbs around them, and one very bright spot on Janice's arm. It wasn't surprising that she would be a focal point of any activity.

The bright spot on Janice's arm. Her mother shields her eyes from the camera flash.

Another photo of Janice and her mother (far right), with Mike and Melissa in the living room. Several photos taken that night showed bright spots near the little girl who used to talk to her "friend" at night.

Bob and Mike set up the infrared camcorders, and both reported some strange sparkling lights and whitish spots darting by—mostly in the hallway. They also both discovered they were experiencing the same feeling in Janice's old bedroom—an uneasiness or nervous energy that was very uncomfortable and took quite a while to shake.

At one point, there were bright lights outside, and we thought another car was pulling in. Actually, it was Barbara's car, which had started by itself and turned on its headlights! Initially, it was rather startling, but she does carry a remote control in her coat pocket, and there was the chance that the buttons were accidentally pushed.

Although that had never happened before, we couldn't say with any certainty that there was something paranormal happening with her car.

Toward the end of the investigation, when everyone was near the living room and Janice's bedroom at the back of the house was empty, I decided to sit quietly and see if anything might happen. In the center of the room, I placed the Trifield EMF meter. It is a much more sensitive instrument than my other EMF meter, and it has the advantage of an audible alarm to let me know if there is unusual activity even when it's too dark or too far away to see. (The meter had been in the room earlier when we first arrived, but nothing happened during that time.)

I settled down and my thoughts turned to the unfortunate accident victim. Less than a minute later the meter beeped softly. I took note of it and assumed it would silence itself in a moment, once whatever had set it off had passed. That wasn't the case. The alarm grew stronger and more persistent—whatever, or whoever, was there wasn't leaving.

I didn't want to move, as that would further disturb the meter (it's that sensitive), but I didn't want to lose the moment. I thought Bob and Mike were in the hallway and softly called out to them. When they didn't respond and the meter started wailing, I realized that subtlety wasn't necessary, and yelled for them to bring the camcorders. They were soon on either side of the room taping in infrared. Several small white spots floated gently near the meter, and then disappeared. We waited to see what would happen next.

As the tense seconds ticked away like hours, I could hear Janice crying in the front of the house. It seemed that as the intensity of the response on the meter increased, so did Janice's distress, even though she did not know what was occurring in her former bedroom. There seemed to be a definite connection, and as much as I wanted to collect data, I didn't want to traumatize Janice. I asked Bob to tell Barbara that it was okay to turn on a light in the living room. Shortly after, she decided to just take Janice outside, and as soon as they left the house, the meter fell silent and whatever electromagnetic field had been present was now gone.

Did the spirit agitate Janice? Did Janice's presence somehow draw the spirit into the house? The dynamics of such a situation are difficult to pin down, but the fact that there was some correlation between the little girl and the unusual activity is not in question.

As it turned out, the prospective tenants did not move in that weekend, and Dan once again made the property available. It's not unusual for such deals to fall through, especially when so many parties and interests are involved. The renters want to make sure they are getting a place that suits their needs and budget, and the landlord wants responsible tenants who will meet their obligations on time. And just perhaps, in this case, there is a third party—a young man who wants to be sure there is some compassionate child with an open mind with whom he can speak, and once again feel as if he is part of the world of the living.

Hopefully, some day he will realize his time on this earth has ended and he will move on. Hopefully, some day, there will no longer be the phantom footsteps down the hall of this Westtown home, no more whitish figures darting about, no more crashing sounds, alcohol smells or other inexplicable phenomena, and tenants will sleep peacefully throughout the night.

This case is a prime example of how tragic deaths leave lasting imprints. Even many years later, innocent people can suffer from such fatal mistakes. Perhaps such spirits return to teach the living important lessons—we are not only accountable for our own actions, we must be ever vigilant that the consequences do not negatively impact others.

It is a responsibility every individual must confront—a very grave responsibility.

The Haunted Daycare

If ghosts are the result of people who die with unresolved emotional issues, then mental hospitals must be fertile ground for restless spirits. If you also consider the "treatments" that were once applied to patients, such as electric shock therapy, insulin induced coma and lobotomy, it becomes even more likely that those subjected to such tortures might not find peace even after death.

When Gina contacted me about strange happenings at a daycare center in southern New York where she worked, it sounded interesting, but when she added that the facility occupied part of a former psychiatric hospital, I knew I had to go. We arranged for Bob and I to visit on an early summer evening. I had basically expected to interview staff members who had experienced potentially paranormal occurrences. It being daylight, with several employees still working in the building, I did not expect to encounter anything unusual. Which just goes to show that even seasoned ghost investigators can be wrong.

Driving into the enormous complex, which is spread over hundreds of acres, is an experience in itself. Many of the buildings are boarded up and overgrown, giving it the feeling of a real ghost town. Even most of the buildings still in use are forlorn looking structures, clearly having seen better days. While there are still several active facilities on the grounds, the entire place is a shadow of its former self, when it was essentially run like a self-sufficient little city. However, the place may not be as empty as it appears, as troubled shadows of former patients may still linger...

When we arrived at the daycare center, I first spoke with Gina's boss, Debbie, about some of the history of the place. She said that the building that housed the daycare center had been the children's dorms, treatment areas and nurses' stations of the mental hospital until 1968. While no children had been housed there since then, the daycare center did once again return children of all ages to the long, dark corridors and small rooms with barred windows. Of course, the big difference with the children there today is that they are not mentally or emotionally disturbed, and will not spend the rest of their lives within those walls.

As to specifics about haunted activity, Debbie told us that a psychiatrist who worked in the building for almost forty years said that so many unusual things had taken place during that time that he had "no doubts" that restless spirits still resided in the old wards of the mental hospital. Given that he is a trained observer of the human mind and understands the difference between reality and imagination, his affirmation makes a powerful statement.

Since the daycare began, many employees have experienced things that cannot be explained. With doors opening and closing themselves, strange sights and sounds, and uneasy feelings being experienced throughout the facility, it is no wonder that the number of eyewitnesses of paranormal events is unusually high. And, in a situation that is rare in most cases, there seems to be general agreement between management and staff that the place is truly haunted by patients who still wait to be released.

Speaking of patients, Debbie also mentioned that several people who had been in the hospital when they were children, had returned years later and told of the drastic measures taken to cope with those who were considered to be out of control. One such method involved submerging children into ice baths, and holding them there until they calmed down. While this hospital did not have the horrible reputation of other institutions like Willowbrook, if forced ice baths were accepted practices, one shudders to think what other abuses might have taken place behind the scenes.

However, even if the best of care had always been administered here, it still remains that there was a constant internal torment suffered by the children who were afflicted with all manner of terrible mental illnesses. Thanks to antipsychotic medications that began to be introduced in the 1950s, many conditions can now be managed, but for much of the twentieth century, the mentally ill were locked away for their entire lives, both behind the walls of institutions and within their own minds.

Before beginning the tour of the facility, Gina and her co-worker Laura told me about an incident that occurred just a few doors down from where we were. During a dark winter's evening, they were taking a break outside on one on the benches. They had a clear, unobstructed view from where they sat of one of the wings of the building, about seventy-five feet away. Suddenly, a strange, blue light was shining in one of the windows. They knew the light was in the bathroom because it was the only small window on that side of the building. It was a bright, intense blue, and the two women watched it in amazement, because no light had previously been on, and no one was in that part of the building.

They went inside to check it out, and found that the dazzling blue light in the bathroom was gone. In fact, it was completely dark, as even the regular white light was not switched on. No one had been in there, the light switch was turned to off, yet somehow an intense blue light had appeared in that tiny children's bathroom.

Others have also reported seeing strange colored lights—even in buildings that have been abandoned and had their entrances sealed. In addition to blue, there have been yellow and green lights spotted. (I was to add to that list of colors with a photograph I took in the attic, but more on that later.)

59

Although as a rule I like to conduct investigations with as few people present as possible, when we began our tour I quickly realized that all the footsteps I heard following us were not of the unearthly variety. Word of the "Ghost Hunt" had spread, and seven or eight employees were joining us to see what we might find. It actually turned out to be helpful, as they told of different things each had experienced.

Our first stop was the kitchen. Laura had experienced cold spots there, and on one occasion, Gina heard something pounding on one of the back doors. While I set up the tape recorder and got the cameras ready, Bob started scanning the area with the EMF meter. Ruling out the areas of identifiable EMF (like refrigerators), there was still a section near the entrance that was giving inexplicably high readings. I decided to set the very sensitive EMF meter on the floor and see what happened. A minute or two passed with no response, but as I started to walk toward the back of the kitchen, taping in infrared, I heard the distinctive sound of the meter's alarm.

The back door of the kitchen.

Hurrying back to the front, I found the group of staff members huddled together, staring intently at the meter that was signaling it had detected something—something that couldn't be seen. As I said earlier, I hadn't expected to encounter anything that day, but obviously someone had other ideas. For several long minutes, the alarm sounded in both short bursts and long periods of activity. While nothing appeared on any of the photographs or infrared video, I was not disappointed by the investigation that had nonetheless started with a figurative bang.

The EMF meter sits on the kitchen floor, while several employees stand in the background listening to the alarm going off.

A literal bang was the subject of our next stop across the hall in the auditorium. One night during a staff meeting in that large, open room, when the rest of the building was locked and empty, everyone heard a very loud banging sound. It seemed to be coming from the hallway right outside the door. Two of the men quickly got up and went to investigate, but couldn't find anything. The entire staff heard it, but no explanation was ever found. This may or may not have any bearing on the strange noise, but adjacent to the auditorium is an abandoned dorm wing, whose entrance in the hallway has been concealed behind a wall. No one can enter that wing, so if the banging had originated from there, it was not a living, breathing person who made those loud sounds.

Inside the auditorium, one of the men pointed out a door leading to a tiny room with an iron ladder mounted on the wall in the back corner. The ladder went straight up through the ceiling the height of two stories, and it was an effort to reach it, especially carrying equipment and squeezing past dusty chairs piled high. With the digital camera around my neck, and an EMF meter in one hand, I began ascending the ladder. I could see a trap door high above me, which most likely went to the roof, but half way up there was a ledge and a steel door. I got that little tickle on the back of my neck, switched on the EMF meter and found that there were some high readings there—and there wasn't any manmade electrical source in this unused portion of the building.

Not knowing what I might encounter behind that door, I didn't climb any higher, but instead pulled open the door with one hand, stuck the digital camera inside, and snapped a picture. A second later, the image appeared on the viewfinder, and I let out a couple of words that will not be repeated here. Even on the tiny one-inch screen on the back of the camera, I could see that I had captured a bright red light up near the rafters of an attic. I quickly snapped another picture, but it was gone.

By this time, everyone back in the auditorium knew I had found something, so I climbed back down and showed them the very unusual object I had photographed. Over the years, I have photographed many white, fuzzy, orb-like balls of light—which I still consider may have natural explanations—but never an angry red light like this. This was one orb that would be hard to explain.

Grabbing more equipment, several of us headed back up the ladder. The unfinished attic was to the left of the doorway, and to the

The bright red orb in the rafters.

right were a couple of small rooms that once held projectors, as the auditorium used to be the hospital's movie theater. In the attic section, the air was surprisingly cool for a hot summer's day, and the projection rooms were also a comfortable temperature. I snapped away with the digital camera, but nothing else appeared. (If dust particles do cause orbs, then each picture should have been full of them up there.)

After poking around for several minutes, I was standing near the door between the unfinished attic area and the first projection room. I was just about to turn to descend the ladder, when I heard very distinct footsteps behind me in the attic. The hair stood up on the back of my neck, and I spun quickly around, but saw no one. Turning back to the projection room, I saw that every living person was accounted for, so it wasn't any of our group who had made those sounds.

I was able to rule out a squirrel or mouse, because with the little bits of debris that scattered the floor, it took the weight of a human to create the distinctive crunching sound that accompanied our footsteps. Even though no one could be seen, something produced sufficient force to make those sounds. Signaling for everyone to be absolutely silent, we waited for several minutes, but nothing else occurred.

Once we came back down, I realized I had not brought the camcorder up, so Bob volunteered to do the infrared taping. When he and three of the group returned to the mysterious upstairs rooms, the EMF readings were gone, and it suddenly felt at least thirty degrees warmer than just a few minutes earlier. When the staff members returned, I could see that each of them was sweating, and they all agreed that it was now brutally hot in the attic and old projection rooms. Bob was up there the longest and the first thing he said as he descended the ladder was, "It *really* got hot up there!" I told him he was not alone in his assessment in the bizarre temperature increase.

So within the span of ten minutes, there were high EMF readings, footsteps, a bright red orb, and air cooler than down in the auditorium. Then there were no EMF readings, nothing appeared in the photographs or camcorder tape, there were no footsteps and the air temperature rose dramatically. It appears that whatever had been causing the unusual activity had gone—and taken its cool air and electromagnetic field with it.

Our next stop was the computer room, which was on the other side of the boarded up entrance to the abandoned wing. I can tell you one thing for certain, ghost hunters do not like sealed entrances to abandoned buildings! However, I wasn't about to start kicking in doors and breaking windows to get inside, so I just had to content myself with stories of the eerie feelings staff members have experienced in the computer room. With all of the monitors throwing out high electromagnetic fields, the EMF meter was useless there, and nothing appeared on any photos. However, there was a door to a closet that was standing wide open that is normally locked. None of our group had been in that room that day, and the only person who might have entered did not have a key for the closet door. Not proof positive of something unnatural, but certainly worth taking note.

What was also worth noting was something that could not be photographed or measured—the prevailing feeling of despair throughout this place, with several spots being particularly intense. Not since spending the night in an abandoned old prison (Eastern State Penitentiary, see story in *Ghost Investigator: Volume 2*) had I experienced such an oppressive atmosphere of desolation, hopelessness and other disturbing elements of dark, negative emotions. Before I had a chance to tell Bob what I was feeling, he turned to me and said, "This is just like Eastern State!" There is some small comfort in the fact of knowing you aren't alone, but an equally unnerving feeling that it is not simply your imagination at work.

Our investigation continued on down what seemed to be a maze of long corridors with small rooms that had multiple doorways. It was sometimes slow going, as every door is kept locked and we would have to wait for the right key to be found, and then the doors would have to be relocked after we passed through. This level of security made it all the more unusual when we heard more stories of doors found standing open, or doors that opened and closed by themselves.

One door that habitually opens by itself leads into the staff lounge. Bob and I both examined the door, and although the locking mechanism doesn't seem to fully deploy, it takes a powerful shove to open. We stood in the hall and tried it several times, and each time found that much more force was necessary than a breeze or even a strong wind to open that heavy door. In lieu of this door with a mind of its own, the staff lounge is not always the best place to go to relax.

Things aren't much better across the hall in the infant room. Motorized baby swings have turned themselves on, and the sight of an empty swing rocking back and forth must be unnerving—especially if you let your mind consider that it is not actually empty! There is a plastic musical ball that also switches itself on, suddenly playing its tune when no human hands are near it. As one staff member said, the tune it plays is "annoying" enough, without the added stress of it deciding to play by itself.

There were some interesting readings in that room, and a general

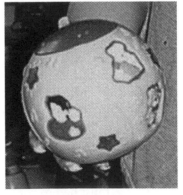

The musical ball.

uneasy feeling. I took a digital image looking down a corridor into the back room of the infant area and saw that there was a very large, bright patch of light against a wall. I took another picture a few seconds later, and the bright patch had moved away from the wall and traveled up the corridor several feet—which meant it was heading straight for me and several staff members standing nearby. That convinced a few of them to get out of the room. I took another picture, and the light was still closer, but much smaller and nearer to the ground. A fourth image showed that the bright light had gone. Perhaps it had passed right by me?

Everyone out in the hallway wanted to see the images, so I switched the camera from photograph mode to playback mode. One of the great things about using digital cameras is the ability to instantly review all of the images stored on its disk. I displayed them one by one, and all of the images came up crisp and clear, which meant that they had been saved correctly on the disk.

However, when I got home and put the disk into my computer, the first two images in that sequence would not display. Somehow, those files had been corrupted, which made no sense since they had been properly saved and I did nothing to try to alter them. So, instead of a great sequence of a large bright light changing size and moving away from a wall of the infants' room and heading straight for me, I have one picture of a small bright spot near the edge of the carpet. Not quite the same visual impact.

Of course, I have had problems with disks before, and images don't always store properly. However, once an image has been saved, and proven to be good by displaying it, I have never had something happen to destroy the image. I guess whatever it was didn't appreciate being photographed.

Further down the hallway is the gym. Several interesting things have occurred in this area. A radio that was once there used to have its volume go up and down by itself. As it was an old radio, they assumed it was broken, so they replaced it. The only problem is that the new radio continued to turn its volume up and down as well. They haven't bothered to try a third radio.

One day when Gina was inside the large, open gym, she was sitting on a bench by the entrance. The door was locked, and no one else was around—or so she thought. It was quiet and the air was still, but then all of a sudden it was like someone had just come through the doorway and walked right past her. It sounded like someone was there, it felt like someone was there, but no one could be seen. Unfortunately for the employees of this facility, it was beginning to sound like this kind of thing was just part of a typical day at the former mental hospital.

At the end of this long, dark wing of the building, was an open play area that was once used to allow patients to get some fresh air, and at least get a sense of being outside. Of course, bars stretched the length of the tall arched openings in the concrete walls, and sunlight through bars does not exactly give the same feeling of freedom. While I didn't find evidence of anything

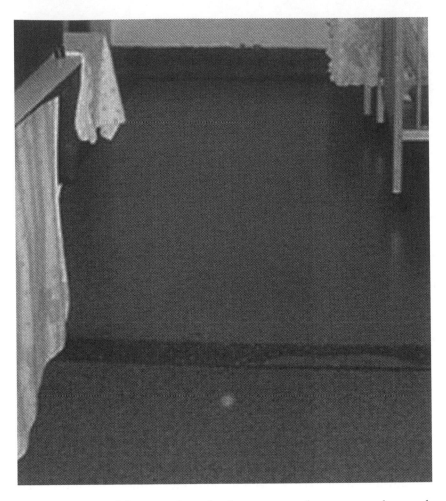

A section of the one photo in the sequence that was not damaged. The bright spot is near the floor by the edge of the carpet.

paranormal in this area, I had to agree with the staff's assessment that this place was "creepy". Even though it was the most open area of the facility, it was here that I had the strongest sense of confinement. I was very happy to leave and go back inside.

We then made our way back to the office area where we began, and I described to Debbie some of the things we had just encountered. She was not surprised by any of the sounds, images, or readings—after fourteen years in that building apparently nothing was surprising anymore!

We packed up our gear and everyone went outside, where we had a brief tour of the grounds around the building we had just explored. We saw an old overgrown playground across the street, and a large, stately building, now boarded up. That building had once been a treatment center for alcoholics and it was definitely one of those places that just felt haunted. I know that's not a very scientific assessment, but just looking at the place made my skin crawl. With so much decay, and the constant reminders of the deepest kinds of despair, you definitely need to have thicker skin than I have to work in such a place.

Both Bob and I needed some time that night to unwind from our encounter, and as the days passed, I thought about everything we had experienced. For me, of all of the unusual and startling things that had transpired, one episode clearly stood out among all of the others. It was nothing I photographed, or heard, or picked up on a meter. In fact, it was nothing for which I could offer any proof whatsoever, but for me, it was the most definitive evidence of lost spirits in that building.

Often when in a haunted location, people get impressions of the presence of someone or something. Those impressions are usually mixed with specific emotions such as sadness or fear, and there can be thoughts and images as well. I have experienced this numerous times, and over the years perhaps I have been able to refine that sense, as I get so many opportunities to use it! It's something I don't always mention unless it somehow relates to other evidence, or is so intense that it cannot be ignored. Under the circumstances, what I experienced that day qualified in both categories.

I was in one of the small rooms and there didn't appear to be any unusual activity of any sort, and I wasn't feeling anything out of the ordinary. As I turned to leave, something suddenly caught my attention in a manner similar to being shouted at by someone just a few feet away, although there were no sounds, lights, cold spots or anything outward. Inwardly, however, I was drawn to an area behind me to my left, between the wall and a cabinet. The area was just about two feet high and maybe a foot wide.

There was nothing visible, but I could sense something like a tiny, swirling tornado. What was even more dramatic was how it felt—as if all of the combined thoughts and feelings of a human being had been thrown into a blender at high speed. I had never experienced anything like it before, as even the most threatening presence is more solid, contained and well-defined. This was chaos, pure mental and emotional chaos.

This is the torment of the mentally ill, I thought, a moment before my rational mind stepped in to suggest that it could be a figment of my imagination. There's this self-governing system of internal diagnostics I always run through on an investigation, which includes frequent reality checks to make sure I'm not taking any little flights of fancy. While I appreciated the moment of reflection, my intuition told me that this was the real deal. Even as I write this a week later, I can still clearly picture the swirling mass of confusion and recall how disturbing and frightening it was to even briefly have such an energy brush against my mind.

67

It was gone as suddenly as it had arrived, and I had to take a moment to clear my head and take a deep breath before I continued. I have encountered spirits who were sad, angry, violent and confused, but never any with this degree of utter turmoil. Just that brief moment has left a lasting impression. It has also helped me better appreciate what private hell the mentally ill endure. If that entity was any representation of what still resides in that daycare building, then it is no wonder that doors open and slam shut, loud banging sounds echo down the corridors and intense lights shine in empty rooms.

If ghosts are the result of people who die with unresolved emotional issues, then this former place of confinement of the seriously mentally ill is a distillery of human misery beyond compare. While there have never been any reports of physical attacks or injuries, I cannot help but think that the presence of such disturbed forces is not the healthiest place to spend five days a week.

However, when the daycare center is filled with the sounds of happy children playing and laughing, it may have some healing effects on the troubled young souls that have remained even after death. Perhaps through these carefree children, the spirits still burdened with illnesses they endured in life will see it is time to let go and move on to a happier place.

If that is not the case for these poor little spirits, then it is a situation too painful to contemplate...

One of the former mental hospital's long dark hallways.

Grandmother's House

Generally, I try to write a story soon after an investigation is completed so all of the details are fresh in my mind. This story is different, however, as almost two years have passed since we first visited this nineteenth century Port Jervis, NY house. A number of unique circumstances have led to this extended time period—first and foremost because it is a fascinating case that called for extra attention.

Another important reason is that we were able to get unprecedented access to this house, as it belongs to the grandparents of fellow ghost hunter Mike Worden. In fact, much of the reason that he became interested in the paranormal stems from a lifetime of experiences in this house. Over the course of several decades, family members have seen and heard things they cannot explain, and they just came to accept that the place was haunted. Kind of puts a new spin on grandma and apple pie...

Unlike some hauntings where there is never a physical appearance, at least one ghost in this house boldly presented himself over thirty years ago. Around 6pm one evening, Mike's mother and grandmother were sitting in the kitchen, where they had a clear view of the front door. Although they didn't hear the door open, they looked up and saw a man standing there wearing a hat and a trench coat. As they had a boarder named Ralph staying with them, they assumed it was just him coming home from work, and they waved to greet him. The man waved back and then went up the staircase to the bedrooms on the second floor. They both commented that it was odd that Ralph didn't come into the kitchen to talk to them as he usually did, but other than that, there didn't seem to be anything strange about the man in the trench coat. Until a few minutes later when the real Ralph walked in the back door.

Realizing that the man in the coat couldn't possibly have been Ralph, that he must therefore be an intruder, the two women became very frightened. They told Ralph what had happened, and he ran upstairs to confront the stranger who not only had the nerve to break into a house with people inside, he had the gall to wave back at them! This was indeed a serious problem, but not the sort they assumed, because there was no one to be found. They searched every inch of the house, but the man had simply vanished. They also discovered that the front door was securely locked, so there would have been no way for him to enter there, and no way for him to come in or leave by any other way without someone seeing him.

Just two years ago, the man in the coat made another appearance. Mike's four-year-old niece was playing in the upstairs bedroom at the front of the house (which over the years has been the location of much of the activity), when she came running downstairs with a look of panic.

"Make the man in the mirror go away!" the little girl insisted.

When asked what the man looked like, she described him as an old man who was smiling—and wearing a hat and a long coat. Once again, no one could be found, but the hysterical girl was adamant about the old man in the hat and the coat, and for months she refused to step foot back in that room.

On another occasion, she saw the man again, only this time he was standing at the bottom of the stairs—exactly where he had first appeared thirty years earlier. In addition to being frightened by this apparition, the girl was also very frustrated that no one else could see him. She was pointing, yelling, "There he is! There he is! Why can't you see him?"

Mike and his sister, Melissa, were there, and the terrified little girl clung to him, continuing to insist that there was an old man in a hat and coat standing there. As they tried to tell her that no one was there, she said that he was going up the stairs, so they followed her as she went after him. The phantom man went into the second bedroom this time, and the girl pointed to the corner and continued to say, "He's over there! Why can't you see him? He's right there!"

Finally, the man vanished from her sight, but the image will probably always be with her. He has not appeared again in solid form to anyone in the last couple of years, but once per generation is enough for any family.

The first bedroom, where the man appeared in the mirror, has always been a room where people have felt uneasy. They feel as if they are being watched, especially at night when trying to sleep. Mike had many firsthand experiences with this feeling, as it was in this room where he sat many afternoons doing his homework after school.

"The desk was in that front room and faced the wall, so when I was working my back was to the room. I recall many times being in there doing my homework and having the feeling that someone was

71

directly behind me—only to spin around to find no one there. I also remember one incident after school when I was watching TV in the living room and I heard a loud thud upstairs, as if the contents of a closet had been emptied in one rapid move. Of course, I ran out of the house and did not go in until my grandparents came home from work!"

That front room also once contained a dollhouse that kept being knocked over, with all of the furniture spilled out across the floor. There was never anyone in the room when it happened, and no reason could ever be found for this sturdy dollhouse to fall over by itself. It happened so frequently, that they finally had to take it away.

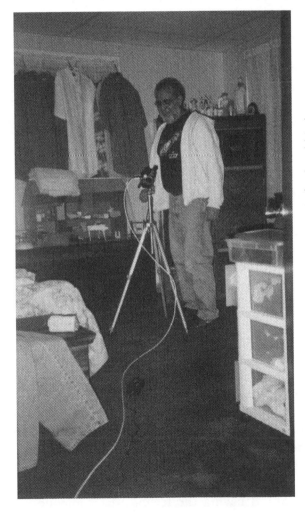

This photo of Bob was taken in September of 2001 in the front bedroom. Note the dollhouse behind him. Also note the drawers that are open on the shelf unit to the right. Family members reported that the next day those drawers were closed and perfectly even, although none of us touched them that night.

The bathroom next to this bedroom has also had its share of unusual activity. Several people have heard footsteps approach the closed door (when they were inside taking care of business), only to open the door and find no one there. Sometimes, those footsteps are accompanied the doorknob rattling, or the shower curtain suddenly flapping as if in a stiff wind, even though the window was closed.

Often when something like that happens, when the unfortunate occupant exits the bathroom there will be the added discomfort of an icy cold presence waiting for them just outside the door. It was no wonder that many family members were very happy when a second bathroom was installed downstairs so they could finally have some privacy!

After years of such experiences, Mike's mother, Linda, tried to make it a policy to never be in the house by herself. Several years ago, a death in the family necessitated that she go and make preparations at the house to receive guests after the funeral. As she drove toward the house, she realized she just couldn't do it alone, so she asked her Aunt Jean and Uncle Bob to join her. It was a good thing, too, because as they stood in the kitchen cutting rolls, the back door kept opening and closing by itself. Jean finally had enough and yelled, "Knock it off! In or out, make up your mind!" With that, the door slammed closed and did not open again.

Unfortunately, this success was short-lived, as this spirit merely decided to change tactics. A few minutes later the power went out in the kitchen. Bob went downstairs to change the fuse that he assumed had blown, but found that the fuse was okay, it was just loose. When he screwed it in tight, the power was back on—but not for long. A few minutes later, the power went off in another section of the house. Again, the fuse was all right, but it had mysteriously been unscrewed like the other one. Linda looked at her aunt and uncle and said, "See? This is why I didn't want to come here alone!"

It is difficult to say if these antics were the result of one of the house's "regular" ghosts, or whether it was the deceased relative dropping in for a few not-so-subtle reminders that *gone* doesn't necessarily have to mean *forgotten*. Two years ago, the entire family witnessed someone else's little reminder during Thanksgiving dinner. As they all sat around the table in the dining room, the door of the china cabinet suddenly opened and a cup flew out and smashed on the floor.

One thing we were later to discover is that whatever spirits linger in this house, they do not appreciate being taunted. Some family members believe that at least one of the spirits (perhaps even the infamous man in the coat) is that of a former owner, a Mr. O'Malley, who lived there sometime during the late 1930s or early 1940s. One evening, Linda's skeptical brother was sitting at the kitchen table and said, "Okay Mr. O'Malley, I'm sitting right here. What are you going to do to me?"

Behind him on a shelf, a set of large ceramic serving dishes slid forward and hit him in the back, but fortunately they were able to prevent them from falling to the floor and smashing. Immediately, her brother announced, "It's okay, Mr. O'Malley, I'm only kidding! I'm only kidding!"

The serving dishes that moved on their own, possibly by Mr. O'Malley?

Interestingly enough, it was Mr. O'Malley who had asked Mike's grandfather not to carry out the extensive changes he had planned. The house had actually been larger, with the back extending out and connecting with the garage. Despite the former owner's wishes, the back rooms of the house were indeed cut off, as renovating and heating

74

the additional space would have been too costly. Also, the removal of that section of the house created space for a yard. Perhaps Mr. O'Malley returned after his death to make sure there were no more alterations to his precious home?

Then there are the upstairs doors that slam when no one is up there, lights that flicker when someone enters the room, a front doorbell that rings when no one is near, and an occasional dog barking—although they do not have any dogs. There are crashing sounds in the kitchen, as if something has fallen and broken, but nothing is ever found. There are sudden cold spots and breezes, and the television turns itself on. Objects placed in one room show up sometimes days later in another part of the house.

So many witnesses over so many years, so many classic symptoms of a haunting—how could a ghost investigator ask for more? And how could a ghost investigator even begin to imagine how much more she would encounter?

One evening in September of 2001, Bob and I met Mike and his friend Autumn at the house. We began by taking a series of photographs throughout the house, and checking for any unusual EMF fields. While nothing of interest appeared in the photos, we did find a very curious phenomenon—a line of high EMF readings that ran from one side of the house to the other. The straight line was roughly two feet wide and was strongest in the front upstairs bedroom. (Note: The dollhouse that kept falling was within the zone of the high EMF.) It continued in the adjacent stairwell, although not as high, and was also detectable in the living room below and in the basement.

Naturally, we assumed it was simply the result of power lines crossing over the top of the house at that point. Easy solution. One little problem. The power lines do not cross over the top of the house. Searching inside and out, we could find no man-made explanation as to why an electromagnetic field bisected this house at that point. However, regardless of our inability to find the cause, the line existed, confirmed by both Mike and I with separate EMF meters. In lieu of this mysterious line, as well as a long history of activity, we decided the front bedroom was a good place to set up the infrared camcorder.

We set it up on a tripod just outside the door in the hallway, and ran a cable downstairs to a monitor in the living room. Mike, Bob, Autumn and I sat in the living room, glued to the monitor, watching for any signs of activity. We saw several of those little white spots moving both super fast and very slow, but they all seemed to be concentrated along that invisible line, which was near the edge of the bed. A few seemed to actually be coming out from underneath the bed, prompting me to comment, "There are monsters under beds, after all!"

Of course, I was only joking; these were no monsters. However, we couldn't be sure *what* they were. As I have stated on previous investigations, insects are easily identifiable, and we could rule them out in this instance. That left dust or other airborne particles, but as Mike said, his grandmother "is a cleaning maniac." Also, no windows were open, and we continued seeing these bizarre little white spots long after we had left the room, giving the air more than enough time to settle. Then there was the fact that they seemed to all either originate along the line or follow its path.

There was another interesting aspect to this—we all were feeling very tense the entire time the camcorder was taping at that angle. However, we didn't realize it until we moved the camcorder farther back into the hallway. There was almost no activity at that point, and it was only then we realized how on edge we had been. Unfortunately, this was only the beginning of the evening's emotional roller coaster ride.

We decided to move the camcorder back to its original position, where it had a better angle on the EMF line, but this time I was going to stay by the camcorder, and Mike and Bob were going to be in the bedroom. As soon as he sat on the bed, Bob commented, "Okay, this is weird." I asked if he was feeling something, and he replied, "Yeah, but I don't know what, though."

That may seem to be a vague answer, but it summed up what we were all feeling. Something, or someone, was there, but it was as elusive as an answer on the tip of your tongue. There was a general uneasiness that was palpable, but none of us could explain why we felt the way we did. As if things weren't strange enough, when we moved the camcorder back a second time, the tension was broken once again. We all went back to the living room to plan what to do next.

Some of the mysterious bright spots actually moved out of the room, through the doorway and across the staircase—all following that line. We noticed this on a couple of occasions, so Mike decided to go back upstairs and position the camcorder so it looked down the staircase. As the mood was light at that point, he decided to have some fun and play to the camera with a Boogie Man face and sounds. Although we had had a good laugh, I also got the distinct feeling something didn't appreciate the humor. Taunting spirits is never a good idea, and my voice is clearly heard downstairs saying to Mike, "Okay, you'll get yours."

In fact, we were all about to get it.

A few minutes later, Bob moved the camcorder to the back wall of the front bedroom, to shoot an angle facing out the door, opposite to what we had been taping. As soon as he got back downstairs, the tape apparently ran out and the camcorder shut itself off. Mike went upstairs to check, and he commented that the mood upstairs was now completely different than it had been at any time that night. The hair was standing up on his body and he was actually feeling threatened.

Even though Bob, Autumn and I were in the living room, we felt it, too. Something was very, very angry, and never before had we experienced such a sense of not being wanted in a house. Now remember, we have been in cemeteries, abandoned prisons, suicide and murder sites, but never before was there such an overwhelming feeling of something wanting us to get out. Although my rational mind insisted that nothing bad was going to happen, the rest of me said the hell with being rational.

Simultaneously, we all decided it was time to leave, and fast. In an unprecedented retreat, we grabbed the equipment and literally ran out of the house. It was not the most dignified way for a bunch of seasoned ghost hunters to leave a haunted site, but the feeling of terror and imminent danger was so extreme, all we could think of was getting out as fast as we could. Again, I must repeat, that had never happened before, and it has never happened since on any other investigation. It was then that I realized the story could not end there. We would have to go back.

Before returning to the house for a second investigation in late August of 2002, we all agreed that there would be no taunting this time. Mike's sister, Melissa, and her boyfriend, Anthony, joined us, and as we began to set up the equipment, we wondered if there would be any activity this time. We soon found out we didn't need to worry.

One amusing moment early on was when I took a photograph of the dining room looking towards the living room and staircase. Bob happened to be standing in the living room, and although he was not the subject of the photograph, he became the object of interest—at least part of him, anyway. In the photo, a large bright patch of light appeared over a rather conspicuous part of his body. Subsequent photos taken from the same location and angle revealed nothing, but we all had a good laugh about Bob and his "affectionate" ghost.

Bob and the curious bright patch of light. Where he is standing in the living room is within the zone of EMF. The front door where the man in the coat appears is behind him. The basement door is on the far right.

We once again set up the camcorder in the upstairs hallway, facing into the first bedroom, with cables running downstairs to a monitor. There wasn't much of interest, until Mike sat on the bed and asked if anyone wanted to make himself known. Immediately, one of those little white spots came zipping past him and out of the doorway. Mike's hair stood on end and he got that spider web feeling all over his skin. There was also a noise in the second bedroom, and I started getting goosebumps.

Things quieted down a bit, and again Mike asked if anyone wanted to communicate. I thought back to the story of the old man who used to live there, and said to Mike, "What was that man's name?"

"Mr. O'Malley," Mike replied, and another bright spot zipped past. Our goosebumps rose to little mountain peaks, and the air grew icy cold. "Mr. O'Malley, it's time to move on."

There were more bright spots, and Bob, Melissa and Anthony said they thought they saw a shadow move across the room as they watched the monitor in the living room. Then there was an odd clinking sound in the second bedroom, and it was so loud that they could hear it downstairs. It appeared that Mike had hit a sensitive note with his appeals to old, dead, Mr. O'Malley.

It was becoming increasingly tense as I stood by the camcorder, watching Mike in infrared sitting in the darkness. He kept rubbing his arms, both to try to relieve that creepy spider web feeling, and to bring some warmth back to his chilled skin, but it wasn't working. As I stood my ground, there was a distinctive sound in the bathroom to my right—something like two pieces of corduroy brushing together. That was followed by a clicking noise directly behind me. Melissa reported that a glider rocker in the living room had started moving back and forth although no one had been near it. It was all very unnerving, to say the least, but Mike had asked for signs, and there's no sense running away from what you ask for.

Things mercifully quieted down for a short while, and Bob came upstairs to check things out. The back bedroom door was closed, and he decided to take a look inside. Unfortunately, he didn't know that there was a rack of shirts just inside the room, and when he opened the door a long-sleeved, white dress shirt swayed in the breeze right in front of him.

"Well, that just gave me a heart attack," he declared, not particularly happy with the fact that he seemed to be the focus of the evening's comedy relief.

However, while he was in that third bedroom, curious little spots seemed to be coming out of the second bedroom. Melissa and Anthony were also upstairs by this point, and everyone agreed that the temperature was dipping once again. It should be noted that Anthony was skeptical about this house being haunted, but even he had to admit to feeling an inexplicably cold breeze on that warm summer night.

Toward the end of the second investigation, I took the top photo. I thought perhaps the bright spot was some type of reflection from the hall light on the ceiling. I switched off the light and immediately took another photo. The spot had changed size and location, but it was still there.

Once again, a sound emanated from the second bedroom, something Melissa aptly described as "like a lid on a jar." If someone was trying to communicate with us, they were certainly using a unique set of sounds. Corduroy rubbing together, clinking, clicking, a jar lid—none of it made any sense, but if its goal was simply to attract attention, it was one hundred percent successful.

We moved the camcorder to the doorway of the back bedroom; Mike stayed alone upstairs to minimize any extraneous sounds. We needn't have bothered, as the noise that was soon produced had enough volume to drown out any of us. As Mike stood in the back room and said the magic words of the night, "Mr. O'Malley?" there was a loud banging on the walls, followed by a heavy thud. Mike yelled, "Oh my God," and quickly retreated downstairs.

"I'm not going back in there!" he insisted, visibly shaken from the unearthly noises that seemed to target him.

After taking a few minutes to catch his breath, and renew his courage, I suggested we both go back upstairs to that most interesting back bedroom. He bravely agreed, and with some natural trepidation we returned. As I manned the camcorder, he once again volunteered to sit on the bed and talk to whoever wanted to respond. While there weren't any more banging sounds, or any unusual sounds for that matter, something else unique began to happen.

We began to feel an overwhelming sadness, and although we were both reluctant to admit it, our eyes were welling up with tears because the feeling grew so intense. Then something even more bizarre happened. As I said to Mike, "I feel like I should say something in French," even though I don't speak the language. I asked if he knew of any French connection with the house, especially in regard to the loss of a child. There was nothing he was aware of, but the impression of the loss of a child and something French grew so strong I needed to step away.

We decided to move back to the first bedroom, but there was no relief to be found there, either. The terrible sadness only intensified, and while I have never personally experienced such a tragedy, I felt the profound grief of a child's death. Meanwhile downstairs, they began hearing noises coming from the kitchen. That was immediately followed by more noises coming from the back bedroom, which was above the kitchen. Things were really heating up—except in regard to the icy temperatures.

Neither Mike nor I could shake the overwhelming sadness, and I could not shake the loss of a child along with something French. Finally, Melissa offered some vital information. She said that when her grandmother was a young woman, she had lost triplets. Two died at birth, but one lived for a couple of days before passing away. That child's name was Michelle.

I shivered as a chilling blast traveled up my spine at the sound of the French name of the little girl who had been lost. That was the answer to the mysterious riddle that had been consuming both my mind and emotions. I had no visible proof to offer, but I knew in my heart that the spirit of the Michelle was still with her mother, who had lost her so many, many years ago. A sad story, indeed, but little Michelle is most likely not alone.

Mike then recalled that his own mother had lost a child, a boy who was buried alongside Michelle. As he told me about his lost brother, there was a tapping sound somewhere nearby, then a few more noises, definitely originating inside the room with Mike.

"Someone's in here," he whispered with growing alarm. "I can hear it!"

Then he experienced "a life-altering sadness" sweeping over him, and he felt like he wanted to cry. In a firm, yet subdued voice, he gently said, "Whoever is here, it's time to let go. It's time to move on."

A moment later, there was a powerful pounding sound on the back of the house. All of us heard it, and even though it was far from the camcorder, it was clearly recorded. There was nothing subtle or vague about this, it was as if something very strong was pounding its fists against the outside wall. This was no baby, and it apparently resented the suggestion of leaving.

Then, emerging from the back bedroom, came the sound of shuffling footsteps moving down the hall—straight toward me. I resisted turning, because I knew there wouldn't be anything visible, but when the shuffling footsteps and strong presence moved within a few feet of my back, I couldn't stand it any longer. I spun around, and of course, saw nothing. At that point, Mike and I both agreed it was time to go downstairs. The oppressive sadness—not to mention the mounting fear—was just getting too much to handle.

However, there was still the basement to explore. After a short break, we moved the equipment down there, and stood in the silent darkness. Almost immediately, the grief and sadness flooded in. This time, it seemed to center around someone different, someone we had briefly had an impression of upstairs. However, the theme of a lost child was the same, as both Mike and I described identical impressions—an older man who had lost a young girl. The clothing seemed to be that of the early part of the twentieth century, and it was not clear to either of us if the girl had died, or had been taken away for some reason. Regardless, the intensity of the sorrow of his separation from the girl who had been his life, felt worse than dying.

Unlike the French name I could not pin down on the child upstairs, this time I sensed the name Rebecca. Was there an older man who once lived in the house, perhaps with his granddaughter, a sweet girl named Rebecca? Had she been taken from him, either by some legal decree, or by a fatal illness or accident? Mike and his family planned to search whatever records were available on those who lived in the house over the century, but their lives were soon consumed with their own personal tragedy.

Mike's grandfather became ill, and he was diagnosed with acute leukemia. It is a painful, debilitating disease, and when death finally claimed him in January of 2003, it was a merciful release.

His grandfather had always joked that if there were any spirits residing in his house, they had not been paying rent and he would kick them out when he got on the other side. Perhaps he has made good on his promise, for since he passed away, the whole family agrees that the house feels different—in a good way for a change.

However, not all activity ceased; most of it shifted to the garage, where his grandfather spent many happy hours tinkering in his workshop. One day, Melissa went in the garage and found that a box of wooden dowels had fallen off the shelf and spilled all over the floor. She returned them to the box, closed the lid, and placed it securely on a shelf. Later that day her father went in the garage and found the same box of dowels open on the floor. He also picked them all up and placed the box securely on a shelf.

Apparently, the third time was the charm, as once again this same box managed to make its way to the floor that day, open and spill its contents everywhere. This final time, her grandmother discovered them and put them back, and they have not fallen since. Another day, her grandmother was in the garage when her husband's shop vac suddenly slid across the floor on its own. While these events are disconcerting, in this light they can also be viewed as attempts to just let loved ones know that someone who cares about them is still near.

With all these reports of new activity and energy shifts, I had to find out for myself, so in July of 2003, Bob and I returned for a third investigation. We were to have our largest group yet—Mike and five relatives and friends—and none of us knew what to expect. As we set up the camcorders and instruments, I wondered if the overwhelming sadness would return, or if the threatening presence would make another appearance. Would there be more information forthcoming on the lost souls that wandered this house, or would there just be another set of mysterious sounds, images and feelings that didn't make sense?

The one thing I didn't expect was nothing—relatively speaking, considering past experience. The place was so unlike it had been that it felt like a completely different house. Not that I was complaining, because what was now absent was everything that had been dark, oppressive and foreboding. There were some inexplicable EMF readings, a couple of orbs and spots on infrared, but the intense spirit of the haunting, so to speak, was simply not there.

The action, what little there was, had also shifted from the upstairs to the living room where the family and friends sat watching the monitors. Several times a chilling breeze curled around them, even though every window was shut in the mid 80-degree weather. At several points, Bob was able to measure as much as a ten degree difference near people who were feeling the cool air, which to the skin felt even colder. It was as if whatever still remained, wanted to be close to these people.

Mike and I discussed the puzzling results a few days later, after we had time to review all the tapes. What seems to make the most sense (which I know is a difficult term to apply to such situations), is that following his grandfather's death, there was some kind of energy shift. Whatever negative entities held sway over the living had gone, or were at least subdued to the point of becoming benign. The positive spirits—most likely actual family members—may still be there, leaving the occasional subtle hint as to their existence.

It seems that the deeper we investigate this house, the more questions arise, but perhaps ultimately it is the process that is most important. There is a lot to learn about life in exploring the mysteries of the dead. The role of an objective observer can only be maintained to a point, because as the sorrow of some distant tragedy touches you in the darkness, you become part of the story, part of the process to investigate, comprehend and give comfort to souls who have not yet found peace.

For at least several decades, this house has been the abode of at least one restless spirit—but there could be many more, over a much longer period of time. Every family has its own heartbreaks and misfortunes that may add layer upon emotional layer to a haunting. A century of tragedies can create a very complex web of energies that a living person may never hope to unravel. And yet, that doesn't mean we shouldn't continue to strive for answers and continue to try to understand our experiences.

In this case, we have had a remarkable opportunity to see that the passing of a loving family member has somehow initiated a drastic softening and shift in the activity. It may be permanent; only time will tell. Regardless, it may indicate a very important factor in this intricate ghost equation—the power of love. Perhaps Mike's grandfather has been able to protect his family one last time, by driving away the negative forces that have been frightening them all these years.

There are many questions that still remain. In time, however, perhaps the identity of the man in the coat and hat will be discovered, the stories of the lost children will be revealed, and things that have gone bump in the night for generations will finally be understood. It is just possible, as this is one case that will never close.

**Late Breaking News **

Just before going to press, Mike called with the following remarkable information I simply had to include.

His late grandfather had a favorite NY Giants blanket that was draped over the back of his chair in the living room. When his grandmother's friend Shirley came to visit, the blanket was put away in the closet of the back bedroom. That night, Shirley slept in the back bedroom, and his grandmother slept on the couch in the living room. When she awoke, the blanket was once again draped over the chair! Both women swear it had been removed from the chair (several family members can also attest to that), and neither of them heard or saw anything during the night. (A photograph of his grandfather that is kept on top of a dresser moves on its own, as well.)

Also, Mike and his grandmother have just begun researching former owners. They came across startling information in the 1909 obituary of Judge Obadiah P. Howell. It stated that he had been predeceased by his seven-year-old son, Bradford, who died of diphtheria in 1892—"from which he never fully recovered from the blow"!

I feel very deeply that this is one the men from whom we received the overwhelming feeling of grief over the loss of his child.

"Fire!"

Late one night during the early 1990s, Alice was suddenly awakened in her Port Jervis home. She was in a cold sweat, because her husband had just yelled, "Fire!" While this is would all be perfectly normal when a house is burning, there were several problems with this event.

For starters, Alice's husband had been dead for several years. Also, even if someone else in the neighborhood had been yelling, she didn't sleep wearing her hearing aid, and therefore would not have been able to hear someone yelling even if he was in the same room, let alone outside. Then there was the fact that Alice's house was not burning. Of course, she quickly went from room to room searching, but did not detect even a whiff of smoke.

Right about now, you are probably thinking it was all just a dream, so what is this story doing in a ghost book? Consider this—at the very moment Alice's deceased husband awakened her yelling, "Fire!" the house they used to live in together on the other side of town was being consumed in a deadly blaze. A man and three of his grandchildren perished in the terrible fire, in the very rooms were Alice and her husband had spent so many happy years.

Not only should this story raise quite a few eyebrows, it also raises some fascinating questions. Did Alice have a psychic experience where she sensed that her old house was burning, and this knowledge manifested into the sound of her husband's voice? Or, if it was truly the voice of her husband from the other side, how come he didn't realize that she was living in a different house, and was not in any danger?

The answer may be very simple. Her husband knew their old house was on fire, and by communicating the fact to Alice that night, at that moment, he was proving that he was still with her, still caring for her, and was still aware of what was going on in the world of the living. In any event, it is startling proof of the existence of the world of the dead. (Before Alice knew about the fire, she told a friend early the next morning about her experience, so she was clearly not influenced after the fact.)

However, as fascinating as it is, the story does not end there. For the past several years, Alice and her friends and relatives have experienced a steady stream of inexplicable occurrences. It's never anything frightening or threatening, just constant little reminders that someone else is there. Appliances and water faucets turn on by themselves. Objects placed in one location show up days later in some other unlikely spot. Her dog stares and reacts to something that doesn't appear to be there. Nothing astonishing, nothing definitive, just things that always make you take notice—which is most likely the point.

Bob, Mike and I visited Alice's place in June of 2003. That evening, she was being visited by her sister, who also related to us some of the things she had experienced. And then there was her friendly Lab mix dog, who was more concerned with getting patted that night, than with the search for spirits. He clearly did not appear to be a dog that became unduly agitated.

We photographed and videotaped a few suspected orbs. Mike thought he had also photographed a blue streak moving behind Alice in the kitchen. We all looked at it on the screen of his digital camera, but when he tried to locate it when he got home, it was nowhere to be found! He even thought that perhaps the streak had simply been me moving in the background (I did have on a blue shirt, although not the same shade), but even then he was unable to find such a photo.

Some of the most compelling evidence was from the EMF meter that I set up in the back bedroom. While we were all sitting in the living room, we heard the meter's shrill alarm begin to sound. Hurrying down the hall, we stood in the doorway and watched the needle sway back and forth for several minutes, before whatever had caused the electromagnetic field had gone. This was of particular interest as I had placed the meter on the exact spot where Alice's husband had died!

Many people might consider the warning voice in the night and all of the inexplicable occurrences to be way beyond the normal world. In retrospect, however, what could be more normal than a husband still watching over his beloved wife? Such things may be difficult to comprehend, but as stories like this continue to surface, it appears as though loved ones never truly leave us. If this is a ghost story, than at least it is not one that frightens, but for once, brings comfort.

Cemetery Gates

In October of 2000, Roxanne Wentworth purchased a brick Cape Cod style house on Middlebush Road in Wappingers Falls, New York. The previous owner had built the house in 1945, and although it needed a little work, the structure was sound. The half-acre property is bordered on two sides by woods, so even though the house sits at a busy intersection, there is a feeling of privacy.

It was nice for Roxanne to have a peaceful retreat, considering that for the last twenty years she has worked for the New York State Department of Corrections. Dealing with a prison environment day after day can be trying, so it was comforting to have a quiet home and a short commute. At least it was quiet and comforting for the first five months.

Roxanne in front of her home.

In February of 2001, Roxanne was putting flowers on a grave at the Wappingers Falls Rural Cemetery, which is several miles from her home. It was early on a snowy Sunday morning, and as she was leaving, something caught her eye. Leaning against the back of a maintenance building was a large pair of iron gates. These gates once

88

stood at the entrance to the cemetery, marking the boundary between the living and the dead. Several years earlier, the gates had been removed and left to rust after a century of service. Roxanne thought they would look great at the end of her driveway, so she arranged to have the abandoned gates brought to her house.

Symbolically, bringing home "a doorway to the dead" might seem to be an unusual thing to do. However, they were strong, heavy, antique gates, made by the Stewart Iron Works of Cincinnati, Ohio (most likely in the latter half of the nineteenth century), and it would be foolish to let superstition prevent such an attractive addition to her property. Yet, some superstitious beliefs have been found to have a basis in fact, and unfortunately for Roxanne, more than the gates were delivered to her home.

The night the gates arrived, Roxanne awoke in the middle of night to the sound of footsteps on the staircase leading up to the bedrooms on the second floor. Her first and only thought was that a burglar had broken in and her life was in danger.

"They were very heavy footsteps, so I knew it had to be a really big man. I only heard the footsteps and creaking boards on the top six stairs, not the entire staircase, which was strange, but I had more important things to worry about. The footsteps stopped when he reached the second floor, and then there was silence. I never felt that kind of fear before in my life, and I just lay there motionless, waiting for my bedroom door to open."

But the door did not open, and no one ever came into the room—at least no one she could see. But someone, or something, did manage to come through that closed door, and what happened next was arguably more terrifying than any attack by a living breathing person.

"Suddenly, something grabbed the hair on the back of my head. I started fighting back, trying to break free, screaming for him to go away and leave me alone, but he was stronger. He was pulling me across the bed, and I felt completely helpless. But when I managed to turn my head, so the area he was grabbing was flat against the bed, he let go. He was gone as suddenly as he came."

When she told her story to a friend, he looked at the back of her head and neck and saw that there were angry red scratches on her skin. This had not been a dream, or part of Roxanne's imagination. Some unseen entity had physically attacked her and left undeniable proof.

One of the pair of cemetery gates.

Now, some people might have had those cemetery gates removed from their property the first thing the next morning, but Roxanne was determined to find out what had happened, and why. Unfortunately, she was to have more opportunities to study the phenomena, as similar occurrences continued night after night. Although they were far less violent—more of taps and smacks—they were nonetheless completely unnerving. She became terrified of spending nights alone in the house, and on one particularly active night she was compelled to leave and stay at a Best Western.

As that would be a very expensive option in the long run, she decided to ask her daughter, Lori, to spend nights with her. For a year, Lori would reluctantly leave her apartment each night to sleep in the house, and while her presence didn't guarantee that nothing would happen, it was at least comforting for Roxanne to know she wasn't alone.

One quiet evening when they were watching television, Roxanne mustered up her courage and decided that for once, she would not ask her daughter to spend the night. Just as she was saying, "I am going to sleep alone," something sharp like a long nail scraped the back of her neck. Quickly she added, "No I'm not! No, I'm not!" and the pain stopped. Roxanne wasn't sure of the motive for the sudden attack, or whether or not some entity wanted Lori there, but it was just another terrifying reminder that sleeping alone was not a good idea.

Word of the haunted house in Wappingers Falls began to spread, and a local radio station arranged to interview Roxanne live on the air. Lori set up a tape so she could listen to the program later. To her amazement, when she played the tape back, there were more voices than those of Roxanne and the show's host. They believe the additional voices were those of the ghosts who wanted to be in on the action. In fact, several times, they have felt that someone was interfering with their telephone conversations, and perhaps this is just one way that spirits attempt to communicate with the world of the living.

Assuming that whatever entities there were anxious to communicate, Roxanne and Lori began to systematically record in various parts of the house and yard, asking specific questions such as who may be there, why were they there, etc. On numerous occasions, they believe they received answers. What sounds like faint voices (and occasionally strong ones, as well) have spoken names and phrases, sometimes with humorous results. For example, in the garage they heard a male voice using some very colorful language. They now refer to him as Robert the Pervert.

The garage.

There is a tree in the backyard that they refer to as the Happy Tree, because of the spirit of a young boy named Dennis, who may be with other spirits of children who seem to enjoy congregating in and around it. A member of a Florida ghost hunting club was filming that tree one night, and he said he captured the image of an ectoplasmic mass moving out from inside the tree, pass in front of it and then return inside.

The "Happy Tree"

There have been many other names and stories, and Roxanne believes that it is "a mixed bag" of spirits that have been drawn by the old cemetery gates. Some, like Robert and Dennis, have more or less taken up permanent residence. Others seem to come and go, and may include local Indians, British colonists, and countless others who have been part of the long history of the area. And if the presence of the gates isn't enough to attract these various wandering souls, there is an old cemetery within sight of their front door, diagonally across the intersection.

However, this nearby cemetery was not the source of any problems with the man who built the house. The man, now in his eighties, came to visit Roxanne and he said that there was never anything unusual in the house for all the decades he lived there. After hearing some of the evidence Roxanne and Lori have collected, though, he is now convinced that the house he built with his own hands has become a home for spirits.

A New York City-based ghost hunting group came to investigate the haunted happenings there as part of a television show produced by PBS. They filmed a mysterious human form moving in the backyard and believed that there is a spiritual gateway between worlds on the property. Remarkably, however, they also concluded that none of the activity was actually centered on the cemetery gates, despite the fact that everything began happening the night the gates arrived! Even in the world of the dead, one plus one should still equal two.

The spirits who visit this place do not appear to be shy about being photographed and recorded, and they also don't miss an opportunity for a party, especially when they are invited. On Thanksgiving morning of 2001, Roxanne went into the basement to do the laundry. (It should be pointed out that she will only enter the basement if her daughter is on the first floor, as she never wants more than one floor separating them at any time.) The laundry was finished early in the day, so she could concentrate on preparing for all the guests coming to dinner.

As she was cooking, she felt as if someone might be present, so she said out loud, "You're welcome to join us if you want. Just give us a sign so we know you're here." In the flurry of activity before dinner, Roxanne forgot about her open invitation, but half way through the meal, Lori asked if the washing machine was running in the basement.

Roxanne reminded her that she had finished the laundry hours ago, and wondered why she was asking.

"Because that's the second time I heard a loud bang down in the basement," she replied. Other guests had heard the noises as well. Apparently, someone had accepted Roxanne's invitation, and had also obliged by giving her the sign for which she had asked.

Several times while sitting in the living room, Roxanne and Lori (who eventually moved in, as she was spending all her nights there) saw a shadowy figure pass through the kitchen toward the dining room. Lori's cat often reacts to something no one else can see. They have photographed many unusual orbs and cloudlike shapes in the house. Cold spots are not uncommon.

"Even with all that goes on," Roxanne said, "most of it is not threatening. But I don't like to say they are positive spirits, because there's nothing positive about what's going on here."

When asked if she has ever told the spirits to just go away, she laughed and simply replied, "Every day!"

Unfortunately, the spirits aren't listening, because activity continues unabated. Between Roxanne, Lori and dozens of relatives and friends, they have collected stacks of photographs and hours of tape recordings. When I arrived one spring evening, I was anxious to see the infamous gates and experience the paranormal phenomena firsthand.

Lori played several of their audio tapes, and there were some of the clearest sounding voices I had ever heard recorded. Roxanne showed me many of the unusual photos, taken both inside and outside. The most remarkable ones were taken by a newspaper photographer who had captured bizarre, multi-colored patches of light in the garage. He stated that in his twenty-year career he had never seen anything like it, and had no explanation for them.

I have to admit I approached the gates with some trepidation, and decided I really didn't need to actually touch them. Photographing them close up would be sufficient. (If cemetery gates could transfer spirits to another location, I didn't want to risk transferring anything to me!)

When it got dark, I started taping with the infrared camcorder. Soon after, there was a definite black object that moved out of the tree and darted behind it, but when I got home and reviewed the tape on the big screen, I saw that I had clearly filmed a bat. Great footage for

Animal Planet, but unfortunately not what I was looking for that night.

However, I did photograph a couple of bright patches of light near the base of the tree, as well as in a few other locations in the yard. It was difficult to say whether or not any unearthly voices were caught on tape, as about six other people had joined us that night, so it was impossible to discriminate between the living and the dead.

I knew I would have to return again, but that didn't prove to be an easy task. Constant rains, sudden illness and scheduling conflicts made it seem as though anything and everything was conspiring against us. Finally, in the middle of the summer Bob and I visited one Friday night. Only Roxanne and Lori would be there this time, but the quiet night for which I had hoped was not quite to be.

It seemed as though it was loud, obnoxious motorcycle night. Then there were the local ambulance and emergency services vehicles that kept wailing by. At one point when I was recording, I asked the spirits to give me a sign. The sudden siren that blasted on a passing police car practically made me jump out of my skin, but it wasn't quite the type of sign for which I had hoped.

It was also difficult to gather any evidence with the infrared camcorder, as the humid summer air was something of a moth, mosquito and firefly soup. Bugs buzzing in front of the lens do not make for a good paranormal investigation.

Then there was the mysteriously bright object I photographed three times in the side yard. It was so highly reflective that I thought it must be a fragment of a mirror or polished metal. We shined our flashlights in the area and carefully walked back and forth, but found nothing. I really thought we had something, until Lori enlarged the image on her computer, and we saw the perfect image of one very large moth, antennae and all. I still don't understand why we didn't see it with our flashlights, or why it was so intensely bright, but unless the spirits were really playing games, it was just an enormous white moth.

I was beginning to think that all the entities drawn by the cemetery gates were intent on not revealing themselves to me. Then we all went in the garage and closed the doors. I was in the front right corner with a tape recorder, Bob was on the left with the camcorder, and Lori and Roxanne stood near the back with their tape recorders. After just a minute or so, there was a distinct plinking or knocking sound near the back wall of the garage, loud enough that both Bob and

I were able to record it. The video showed that neither Roxanne nor Lori had moved, and the sound had clearly originated behind them.

Then there was the sound of something tapping on the long extension ladder hanging up on the wall next to me. It was in this area that the newspaper photographer had captured some of the multi-colored lights. I asked if anyone else was hearing it, and although it was clear and distinct to me, no one else could hear it. That meant it had to be very close.

Again, the videotape revealed nothing, but my tape recorder did record the sounds. They were unmistakable—light tapping on the hollow aluminum rungs of the ladder. I tried to imagine some large bug banging against the ladder possibly making that sound, but still nothing showed up on the videotape.

The noise continued, and drew closer to me, and this time I did jump out of my skin as something light and feathery brushed along the length of my arm. I suppose it could have been another large moth—a relative of the huge white one in the side yard—but when I turned on the lights, we couldn't find any insect in there capable of either tapping on a ladder, or brushing such a large area of my skin. It was a tantalizing event that convinced me that further investigations would be needed.

In the six or seven months since I learned about this case, many people still ask why Roxanne and Lori don't simply remove the cemetery gates. It sounds like a simple solution, but this may be a far more complex situation. Roxanne is concerned that taking away the gates might permanently trap the entities on her property—and make them very angry—and that's the last thing she wants to do.

The ladder on the wall of the garage.

96

It seems as though the spirits who come and go, and those who have stayed, all have some connection, perhaps sudden or tragic deaths. Perhaps these gates are their last entrance to this world where they try to seek the peace that has eluded them in death, and therefore, the gates may be serving a very necessary function.

Fortunately, there will still be plenty of time to study this fascinating case. Roxanne and Lori do not plan on moving any time soon, the cemetery gates are going to keep standing at the edge of their driveway, and the numerous ghosts who walk the grounds and dart around inside the house don't seem too anxious to leave, either.

In any event, this case is an excellent example of being careful about what you bring into your house. Even if something is free, with no strings attached, it doesn't mean there aren't any spirits attached...

The infamous moth, with Bob in the background. Even though we were able to copy the picture to Lori's computer, when I got home, I kept getting a file error for just that picture. I gave up, and asked Roxanne to email it to me. Then I decided to try the disk one last time, and up came the photo with no problem! A technical glitch and a coincidence? Perhaps, but if anyone sees more than a moth in this picture, let me know.

To order books, get info, and share your haunting,
contact the Ghost Investigator through:

www.ghostinvestigator.com

Or write to:

Linda Zimmermann
P.O. Box 192
Blooming Grove, NY 10914

Or send email to:

lindazim@frontiernet.net

Copy this page to use for your own ghost hunt. If you know of a haunted site you think should be considered for an upcoming book, please contact me at:

P.O. Box 192, Blooming Grove, NY, 10914

www.ghostinvestigator.com

Field Report

Date: Location:

Time In: Weather:

Names of People Interviewed:

Equipment: Camera ☐Video   ☐ Tape Recorder ☐
                      Thermometer   ☐   Other:

Experiences: Sounds   ☐ Odors   ☐ Cold Spots ☐
       Visuals ☐Touch/Sensations ☐Movement   ☐

Details (Attach extra sheet if necessary):

Time Out: Total Time on Site:

Conclusions:

Prepared and Signed by:

Witness(es):

Other books by Linda Zimmermann

Look for Linda Zimmermann's new ghost novel in 2003.

Science Fiction Novels

Mind Over Matter   Ten wealthy, powerful members of the Upper Circle rule the Union with an iron fist, and a small chip implanted in every citizen. Born to the privileged class, Walter Danan is now a wanted man. He has discovered extraordinary powers with which he hopes to break the council's grip and set mankind on a higher path of *Mind Over Matter*.
          "Classic space opera!" Ernest Lilley, Editor, *SFRevu*

Home Run   On the fast track to becoming a baseball superstar, Rick Stella's injury leads him to join the Pioneer program for a year-long mission. Pioneers are sent into the farthest depths of space to start colonies, and are often never heard from again.
   When Rick becomes marooned with his android crew, he must decide whether he is willing to sacrifice his dreams, or risk everything trying to make it home.
"Linda Zimmermann shows why she's an All-star in combining a story about baseball & SF to remind us how to overcome obstacles to emerge a winner!"   **Tony Tellado, *Sci-Fi Talk***

History

Civil War Memories "An exciting compilation of vignettes which bring Civil War history alive."   Alan Aimone, USMA
                                                              West Point

Forging a Nation   "Linda Zimmermann blends the history of a single family with the history of our nation in its formative years. This is a story of patriotism, privilege and tragedy which touches the heart, and gives the reader a fascinating and very personal window into the past."
          William E. Simon, former U.S. Secretary of the Treasury

"A worthy book."   Arthur Schlesinger,
                                    Pulitzer Prize winning author/historian

** Special Last Minute Addition **
to "Grandmother's House"

Literally hours before the completed manuscript was to be mailed to the publisher, Mike Worden emailed me the following pictures and additional information. It was too late to incorporate this into the body of the text, but until the ink hits the paper you can always add another page to the back of the book.

As I indicated with the brief addition to the end of the story "Grandma's House", Mike had just found some remarkable information about a former owner, Judge Obadiah P. Howell, who had been devastated by the loss of his son, Bradford. For the remaining seventeen years of his life, he was never able to overcome his terrible grief. This is exactly the type of feeling we had experienced during an investigation—a feeling Mike had so accurately described at the time as "a life-altering sadness."

It was also learned that Judge Howell was a powerful advocate for children, and devoted much of his life to their welfare. Even though he had lost his own son (or perhaps as a result of the tragedy), he focused his energies toward improving the lives of other children.

Clearly, this man fit the emotional profile of the haunting, yet the question remained—did his features fit the physical profile of the apparition? Mike and his sister, Melissa, went to the local historical society to try to find a picture of the judge. They searched through many books but came up empty. Finally, one of the volunteers suggested a huge volume on Orange County history.

Removing the massive book from the shelf, she placed it on the table and randomly opened it to a full-page picture of a distinguished looking gentleman—who just happened to be Judge Howell! The woman was astonished, and repeatedly said, "Oh my, that's him isn't it? Oh my!" A buzz went through the room, as everyone knew why they were searching for the picture. When this woman took down the enormous volume and opened right to the picture of the judge, skeptics became believers on the spot. And when Mike showed a copy of the photo to his mother, she said that he looked like the apparition of the man she had seen (without the mustache) so many years ago!

As incredible as this story continues to be, it doesn't stop there. Mike then went to the Laurel Grove cemetery to find the Howell gravesite. While the actual graves did not produce any surprises, their location did.

In June of 2001, Bob, Mike and I had conducted an investigation of the cemetery (see *Ghost Investigator: Volume 1*). There was one area where Mike previously had something bang on his car. When we went back to that location, both he and Bob experienced an intense, skin-crawling sensation. We had concluded that this area was extremely active—and it is there that Mike just discovered that the Howell family is buried! We had no idea who the Howells were at the time, but we certainly do now!

I am still in awe of the many layers of this haunting that have peeled away and revealed themselves, but I have no doubt there are more surprises in store for us at Grandma's house…

Judge Obadiah P. Howell

From left to right: Mrs. Frances Howell, Bradford, Judge Howell.

Lightning Source UK Ltd.
Milton Keynes UK
UKHW011303300920
370796UK00001B/49

9 780971 232624